Chukwunyere Duruh-John
A Real View of
BOB MARLEY
through Inspiration

First Printing: 2015

ISBN 978-3-00-048448-3

Chukwunyere Duruh-John
Hauptstr. 23
D- 74821 Mosbach

ajculture[AT]gmx.de
www.2000yrs-of-history.de

The playlist: reggae-African Jamaican Culture

It's a special edition of the playlist, with Chukwunyere-Duruh-John picking eleven songs to soundtrack this new book, A Real View of BOB MARLEY through Inspiration. You may listen to the songs in the playlist at http://www.2000yrs-of-history.de/musikger.php | http://www.2000yrs-of-history.de/musikger.php | **Song Lyrics in the book.**

Playlist:
1. Bob Marley
2. Rastafari pray
3. Zion Train
4. Zion
5. Jah made us
6. Carry on Rastaman and Rastawoman
7. Mud House
8. Mosiah Marcus Garvey/Africans Unite
9. Jah call all
10. Ungodly Nation
11. Roots of Haile Selassie I Rastafari

Youtube: **https://www.youtube.com/user/africjam9**

SYNOPSIS

Robert's life had a very uncanny resemblance with the history of world's greatest reggae maestro **BOB MARLEY** with whom he shared identical name.

He was born of a teenage mother and illegitimate elderly man. Abandoned by the father and struggled in poverty while living in a poverty ridden part of town.

So fascinated by this immortal man, he fashioned and modeled his life around him and even went as far as wanting to look exactly like him.

He performed his music and did all sorts of things to raise money for plastic surgery that will turn him into the world's greatest reggae idol...**ROBERT NESTA MARLEY**.

PLOT

Robert works in a downtown studio as a studio session musician; that was the life he knows working six to six (6 to 6).

LOVE CALLS...One day, Rita his girlfriend wanted to know why he lives the way he does and he sits her down and takes her on a journey of his reason... His desire to be like the only man he ever loved, adored, worshipped and desired to one day be like.

She also found out that his major reason for wanting her was because of her name **RITA**...the name of Bob Marley's first wife and possibly first love. Answers; she was astounded to hear.

ENJOY THE RIDE...

CHARACTER ANALYSIS

1. **Bobby: Athletic and handsome…African male**
    Kind hearted, extremely gifted and highly cultured…
    dreadlocked with lots of vision and growing ambition to be like
    the man he ever loved; **Bob Marley**. He reads books written
    about him all the time.

2. **Rita: Slim, beautiful, African Female**
    With a glamorous touch of modernity, she is a sucker for true
    love and romance, still believes in happy endings and Florence
    Nightingale, she was a perfect girl for Robert.

3. **Peter: African male**
    Semi- educated bully; he has the attributes of greatness but was
    too lazy to really make anything out of his life; violent and
    short tempered, he is a damn good artiste that could sing any
    song even when his eyes are closed.

4. **Bunny: African male,**
    Educated; he has the attributes of greatness too, he was an
    idealist who lived by his beliefs and maxims. Struggled to
    make something out of his life; jolly good fellow, he is a damn
    good artiste that could sing any song even when his eyes are
    closed.

    OTHERS COME AS THE STORY GOES

SHOOTING DRAFT

OPENING SEQUENCE

COPTER AERIAL SHOT OF JOHANNESBURG AT SUNSET

FADE TO…

JOHANNESBURG INNER CITY. A PARK BY A ROAD SIDE, CHILDREN PLAYING SOCCER, OTHERS WATCHING… 5 P.M

CUT TO:

LONG SHOT – SAME LOC

Scene 1:   Estab shots
Ext.
A group of young men sit at a nearby park smoking herb;

Enter the sound of siren…they look up.

CREATIVE SHOT – DIFFERENT LOC

A Police car speeds down the road on its business… they run and disappear down the street.

Cut:

NEXT DAY –
TIME… 10 a.m
We hear the sound of guitar and a young man singing…

CRANE SHOT: UPTOWN BUILDING….BRAAMFONTEIN

MIX WITH A STREET SHOT OF JOHANNESBURG WITH ITS BEAUTIFUL STREETS AND ROBOTS.

START CREDIT SEQUENCE

FADE TO…

ROOF TOP OF A HIGH RISE BUILDING.
QUICK SHOT OF…

BOBBY IS SITTING IN A CORNER; STRINGING HIS GUITAR AS HE SINGS….**BOB MARLEY**

Scene 2:   Ms/ cu shots
Ext:
Snapshots…camera moves from a round piece of wood; on it is a small portion of herb; finished rolled spliff and a lighter…
It goes on a tight close-up shot of hands beating a conga drum…
Then of a mouth humming a song…
Slow pan. Camera opens on slow rhythmic movement to reveal three (3) young men in a music band doing rehearsals…

Feed to black

Feed in…
Scene 3:   Creative shot
Ext:
Camera pans from a bottle of vodka sitting next to a pair of legs, it gradually moves to tight C.U shot of the hands stringing the guitar cords…

Enter… the sound of the guitar as he starts **Bob Marley.**
Move to a C.U shot of the mouth as he starts to sing the lines…

BOBBY
Everybody has to know o
HAS TO KNOW O; HAS TO KNOW O
Who Bob Marley is
RIGHT NOW

Everybody has to know o
HAS TO KNOW O
Who Bob Marley is
WHO BOB MARLEY IS

Everybody has to know o
HAS TO KNOW RIGHT NOW
Who Bob Marley is
WHO BOB MARLEY IS

Everybody has to know o
Who Bob Marley is
The young gonna know o
Who Bob Marley is

WHO BOB MARLEY IS
The young gonna know o
Who Bob Marley is
The old gonna know o

RIGHT NOW
Who Bob Marley is
HE TROD ON THE ROAD I AND I WALK
The old gonna know o

Who Bob Marley is
Easterners gonna know also
Who Bob Marley is
WHO BOB MARLEY IS

Easterners gonna know o
Who Bob Marley is
Westerners gonna know o
Who Bob Marley is

HE PAVED THE WAY
I AND I TROD ON
Westerners gonna know o

Who Bob Marley is

Northerners gonna know also
Who Bob Marley is
Northerners gonna know o
Who Bob Marley is

Southerners gonna know o
Who Bob Marley is
Southerners gonna know o
Who Bob Marley is
Everybody has to know o
RIGHT NOW
Who Bob Marley is
WHO BOB MARLEY IS

Everybody has to know o
Who Bob Marley is
HE PAVED THE WAY
I AND I TROD ON

Everybody has to know o
Who Bob Marley is
Everybody has to know o
Who Bob Marley is

Brings Bobby into view as he continues singing…

BOBBY
The twentieth century Jah Rastafari prophet
Was born up the mountains of Nine Mile
In the Parish of St. Ann, Jamaica
GREETINGS JAMAICANS GREETINGS
He was a Rastaman
From the tribe of Joseph
He chant about Africa Unite
Natty dread, So Jah say
He chant down Babylon

Everybody has to know o
Who Bob Marley is
WHO BOB MARLEY IS

Everybody has to know o
Who Bob Marley is
Everybody has to know o
HAS TO KNOW O; HAS TO KNOW O

Who Bob Marley is
WHO BOB MARLEY IS
Everybody has to know o
Who Bob Marley is

Americans gonna know o
Who Bob Marley is
Americans gonna know o
Who Bob Marley is

Europeans gonna know o
Who Bob Marley is
Europeans gonna know o
Who Bob Marley is

Asia people gonna know o
Who Bob Marley is
Asia people gonna know o
Who Bob Marley is

Africans gonna know o
Who Bob Marley is
Africans gonna know o
Who Bob Marley is

I and I know o
Bob Marley
Every Jah Jah children Know o
Bob Marley

Future generation know o
Bob Marley
Future generation know o
Bob Marley

Everybody has to know o
HAS TO KNOW O
Who Bob Marley is
The King of Reggae
ROBERT NESTA MARLEY
Everybody has to know o
Who Bob Marley is
Everybody has to know o

Who Bob Marley is
Everybody has to know o
HAS TO KNOW O
Who Bob Marley is

Everybody has to know o
HAS TO KNOW O; HAS TO KNOW O
Who Bob Marley is
Everybody has to know o
Who Bob Marley is

Everybody has to know o
HAS TO KNOW O; HAS TO KNOW O; HAS TO KNOW O
Who Bob Marley is

Everybody has to know o
Who Bob Marley is

[Guitar Cords; :| Em Em | D D | Hm Hm |:]

Fade to:
Sound of music…
"Rastafari pray" by African Jamaican Culture

Song;
Rastafari
Pray for I
Let I hide
Myself in thee

Let the righteous
Stand on top
And the wicked
Come repentance

Rastafari
Pray for I
Let I hide
Myself in thee

Let the righteous
Stand on top
And the wicked
Come repentance

No truer statement has ever been made
Than that which was written
In the book of life;
In the book of roots;
It was;
Man Know Thyself;
Man Know Thyself;
Those who love I
Jah bless them
Those who hate I
Jah forgive
For they know not
What them doing
For they know not
What them doing

Rastafari

Pray for I
Let I hide
Myself in thee

Let the righteous
Stand on top
And the wicked
Come repentance

Rastafari
Pray for I
Let I hide
Myself in thee

Let the righteous
Stand on top
And the wicked
Come repentance

Rastafari
Pray for I
Let I hide
Myself in thee

Let the righteous
Stand on top
And the wicked
Come repentance

Rastafari
Pray for I
Let I hide
Myself in thee

Let the righteous
Stand on top
And the wicked
Come repentance

[Guitar Cord; ||: G| G ||: D | G :||]

Scene 4: Ms/ cu shots
Street downstairs, rows of passing cars…Rita emerges from an adjoining shop into the street, calls Bobby from her cellphone.

Cut:

Scene 5: Ms/Cu shots
Back at the roof top, Bobby is still playing music on the guitar…his phone rings; he picks and checks caller ID.

BOBBY
Yes, my beautiful. I'm in my sanctuary

Scene 6: Ms / mid shot
Street downstairs, Rita is on the phone while walking.

RITA:
Oh! Ok…I'll be there now

Camera pans around on exterior shots of the surroundings in quick snap shots…zooms in on a door handle, Peter enters carrying a plate of food wrapped in plastic..

Peter: Talks to Bobby
Ol' boy, let's eat

Bobby: **turns and looks at him**
What did you buy?

Peter:
What did you expect?
(He brings out the food and they eat)

Rita enters…

Rita: Greets
Hi people…

Bobby:
Masheri

Peter:
Eta!

Rita: Hugs Peter; goes and kisses Bobby…**stands next to him.**
Still busy?

Bobby:
Not really; come and get some food; we'll go immediately after

Rita: shakes her head
No…I'm fine

Bobby: shrugs his shoulder
Ok…I'll eat for the two of us

Fade to dark

Scene 7:   ws/sf
Int:
Another part of town, a lazy street
Change of music
Shot of a High rise block of flats
Fast zoom to a window from an external shot
Camera goes inside…shows time on the wall clock.

Inside… Bobby and Rita are seated on a sofa, Peter comes from the inside, walks across and leaves for the studio.

Peter:
I'll see you love birds later…

Rita:
You just came in, where are you bound?

Peter:
Studio…I got a session

Bobby: waves
Adios…see you soon

Peter: leaves
Sharp… see you then

Exuents…

Rita: turns to Bobby, begins to stroke his hair…
I've been meaning to ask you this Honey.

Bobby: looks at her
What is it Baby? …Anything the matter?

Rita:
No…no…no my baby…it's just

Bobby: overlaps, interjecting.
What is the problem; don't make me nervous…you know you women know when to throw the sucker punch.

Rita: surprised
Hawu…where did that come from; is there anything I should be nervous about?

Bobby:
Anything like what?

Rita:
You tell me

Bobby:
Nope… relax, there is nothing.

Rita: relaxes
Ok then; I just wanted to know…
(She stops on noticing how he is looking at her anxiously)…what?

Bobby:
What?

Rita: smiling
Why do you love Bob Marley so much?

Bobby: exhales
Is that the question…oh! My God, I thought there is some serious
stuff.

Rita: laughing
Stuff like what?

Bobby:
I don't know…women issues

Rita:
Issues like what?

Bobby:
I don't know…you know they never end

They begin to laugh

CUT TO:

Scene 8:   w/s
Ext:
An early morning shot of Johannesburg waking up;
Rea vaya buses loading and moving.

Mix shot:
Gautrain on cruise from Johannesburg to Pretoria; see professionals get in and out of it…

Quick dissolve.

Window of an up market office and/or studio.

Show time…9 a.m

Cut to:

Scene 9:   s/s
Int.
The studio is in session, Peter is singing; the studio engineer is at the console along with two others...
Bobby enters, begins to greet. Zachy the studio engineer over hears **African Jamaican Culture's "Bob Marley"** playing from his phone and comments.

Zachy: Shaking his head to the beat
Meenn!!...Waoh! What a song to start the day with.

Bobby:
This is who I am

Zachy:
Who are you? Bob Marley?

Bobby: smiles
Physically, no…spiritually, yes

Zachy: Frowns
Now that's confusing

Bobby:
Put it this way; he was everything I want to be and may ever be…and more…

Others watch in fascination

Zach:
Wow! …More confused

Bobby: relaxes
You know what…let's work, you'll realize very soon.

Zach:
If you say so

Enter music
Bobby goes to the singing booth…begins to sing another African Jamaican Culture's song; Zion Train

Zion Train
Jah Jah train
To Zion
Get on board

Only the clean hands
And pure in heart
Will enter
Only those can get on board

Zion Train
Jah Jah train
To Zion
Get on board

Only the clean hands
And pure in heart
Will really enter
Only those can get on board

Zion Train
Jah Jah train

To Zion
Get on board

Only the clean hands
And pure in heart
Will enter
Only those can get on board

Zion Train
Jah Jah train
To Zion
Get on board

Only the clean hands
And pure in heart
Will really enter
Only those can get on board

Zion Train
Jah Jah train
To Zion
Get on board

Only the clean hands
And pure in heart
Will enter
Only those can get on board

Zion Train
Jah Jah train
To Zion
Get on board

Only the clean hands
And pure in heart
Will really enter
Only those can get on board

[Guitar Cords; A- | Dm]

Fade to dark

Scene 10:
Ext: Balcony of a house
Rita and two (2) friends are seated there; they mock her about her
wanna-be super star boyfriend whom they see as a nerd who leaves a fake
life because of imitation of Bob Marley. They are laughing heartily while
mocking her.

Rita: continues to argue extensively.
You people don't know what you're talking about, moreover. This is
a free country that guarantees us freedom to be whomever we choose to
be.

Lebo: laughing mischievously
You're correct **(sarcastically)**

Tina: also laughing
Ya…freedom for some little madness.

Rita: angry
Be careful what you say; you have no right…

Lebo: tries to pacify her
Come on now Sis…you know we're only joking

Rita: retorts
Joking my foot; you should for once think of better things to joke
with.

Tina: rubs her shoulder; apologizing
Sorry now…hm? Forgive and forget

Rita:
You think everything is funny; you should be ashamed of yourselves.

Lebo:
Really?

Rita:
Really

Cut to:

Scene 11:
Ext.
MASTER SHOT – SAME LOC
Aerial montage shot of the city depicting time of day.

5 p.m.

Dip to black

Scene 12:
Int: studio
Bobby and friends finish for the day…

Bobby:
The day was cool; time to go

Peter:
Yebo…I'm going too. The day was kind.

Bobby: asks Zachy
Are you coming Zachs?

Zachy: talks from the booth
Ya… let's go

Bobby makes for the door; others follow, they walk down the corridor out of camera shot.

Cut to:

Scene 13:
Int:
Bobby's house, Rita is watching television and eating popcorn. Bobby enters…

Bobby: drops his bag on the kitchen deck…speaks to her.
Ola Masheri
Goes to the fridge

Rita: replies
Hi Baby; how was your day?

Bobby: takes a bottle of water
Hectic

Rita:
Really?

Bobby:
Ya…very hectic
Goes and sits next to her on the couch, begins to eat the popcorn too.
What's for dinner?

Rita:
Let's eat out ne?

Bobby: nods in the affirmative
Cool…even though there is nothing better than home-cooked meal.

Rita:
We can buy and eat from home then

Bobby: raises his hand in resignation
Whatever you want Masheri

Rita: gets up
Lets go…its what I want
(Takes his hand)
Let me go and spoil you a little

Bobby: gets up and follows her
Ok Masheri…whatever you say

They leave

Cut to:

Scene 14:   w/s c/u
Ext:
A broken down courtyard, Zachy and the boys are busy smoking herb and discussing purchase of stolen cars.

Zachy:
Meen! …You people are not it anymore…what's up with that?

Fats:
Hei Boss…we can't find that car; man!!...its too hot now. eish!

Tiny:
Yo! …We're trying very hard Bossman, I promise you.

Zachy:
Well…you need to try harder people. My contact in East Africa is seriously on my neck and you know its too much money in dollars.

Tiny:
Ya…dollars; that money is too much; man!...

Fats:
You get a little, its too much Rands.

Zachy:
I'm glad you know that, get me the car men and get yourselves too much dollars.

Fats:
Sharp Boss

Tiny:
We'll get it Bossman

Zachy:
How soon?

Fats:
Now…now

Zachy:
I hope so

Tiny:
Believe so Boss

Cut to:

Scene 15:
Int:
An empty lounge, the door opens from outside; Bobby and Rita enter, carrying plastics of drinks. They put them on the table, takes the one they want to drink, sits down and begin to drink.

Rita: mischievous
Can I ask?

Bobby:
Don't start now…your questions are normally poisonous

Rita: shocked, exclaims
Poisonous?

Bobby:
Yes…you know what I mean

Rita: takes his hand
Baby…you'd wanted to tell me why you love Bob Marley so much.

Bobby:
Oh!...is that your question?

Rita:
Ya

Bobby:
Easy…for starters, he was born like me.

Rita:
How do you mean, born like you?

Bobby:
Ya…poor, wretched, insignificant and by a teenage mother without a husband by her side…

Slow dissolve; along with his voice.

**Aerial shot of…St. Ann Parish; Nine Mile Village; Jamaica
One in a row low cost buildings…**

Scene 16:   ws/mid shot

A young pregnant woman lies on an iron bed. She is attended to by a midwife; she is in labor and giving birth to a baby…a male child who turns out to be Robert Nesta Marley. (Bob Marley)…the baby is born.

Cut to:

Scene 17:   mid shot
Int:
Bobby's flat, he is with Rita to whom he is narrating the story about the things he learnt about Bob Marley.

Bobby:
I was born in similar circumstances many years later; thousands of miles away from St. Ann's.

Slow **dissolve**

The suburb of Malvern in Johannesburg. A run-down house, inside she is in labor, she is attended by a mid-wife who helps her deliver a baby boy.

Scene 18:   wide shot
Int:
Rita is fascinated by what she heard' she urges him to tell her more.

Rita: fascinated, she pretends not to be.
Waoh! …is that all or there is more of your obsession with the man?

Bobby:
Obsession…I am not obsessed with anyone; he is just my idol, role model and someone whom I value more a father I knew very little about.

Rita:
Be careful what you say; be careful how your mind works. This is a dead man we are talking about.

Bobby:
Yes; but he lives in my head…in everything I do. He lives in me.

Rita:
It sounds spooky when you say that; just because you were born alike does not mean that a dead man lives in you.

Bobby:
You think that is all?

Rita:
What else?

Slow dissolve

Back in St. Ann; young Marley and Bunny Wailer learns to play the guitar…

Mix with

Voice over of young Bobby and Zachy learning to play the guitar too.

Voice over…
My life took a very similar track as was that of a man who died many years before I was born. Could that have been just a co-incidence.

Cut to:

Scene 19:   Estab/mid
Int:
Back at Bobby's flat, Rita is still awed by the things Bobby is telling her.

Rita:
Crazy…seriously crazy. How sure are you of these things you are telling me. This man died many years before you were even born.

Bobby:

Which makes it all the more interesting.

Dissolve to:

Voice over

Growing up wasn't easy at all; poverty was everywhere in our lives; his growing up in Trench town was similar to my growing up in Hillbrow where crime and brutality reigned obviously empowered by prevailing poverty and degradation of human values.

Slow dissolve…

Create scenarios to depict ghetto life; hardship in a poverty and crime ridden neighborhood.

Cut to:

Scene 20:

Ext: Ws/mid/sc

Scenario one…

Two (2) young boys walk down a lazy street;

flanked on either side of the street are groups of young gangsters sitting on pavements and/or lazying about for nothing.

One of the two (2) boys is Bob Marley, he has a ball in his hand. They see an old lady selling cakes at an intersection; goes to her, one engages her; the other steals some of the cakes and they run down the street pursued by some boys on a pavement who saw what happened.

Over the voice over; show a video of Trench town then and possibly now. Juxtapose with Hillbrow then and now as well on a split-screen format.

Slow dissolve…

Scene 21:   L/s mid/cus
Int.
Scenario two…

The two boys are kneeling before a very angry woman carrying a whip; she reprimands them for stealing cup cakes, reminding them they could be killed for a much lesser crime.

Lady:
What were you thinking?...ehe?...what is wrong with you boys?
You want to bring shame on me?
You want to die?
People are killed for lesser crimes in this God's forsaken neighborhood
(She flogs them on their hands; the boys cry)

Little Bobby: protests
we were hungry Mum

Lady:
I gave you cookies for breakfast...what else do you want?...a cow.

Little Pete:
Sorry Ma...we'll not do it again

Lady:
No, you'll not...because I'll skin you alive before you get us all killed.

(A huge stone lands on their glass window shattering it; shattering it...they look out through it and sees two boys running down the street;

Bobby reacts angrily.

Bobby: angry
I'll kill them

Lady: **shouts at him immediately**
That's what happens when people steal...they loose respect. We'll go now and apologize to the lady and pay for the cup cakes...you boys will then work and pay me back the money.

Get up and let's go

(They leave)

Cut to:

Scene 22:   Estab/mid.cus

Ext:

The lady and the boys are with the cup cake lady…

Enter background music

They apologize for stealing the cup cakes.

Little Bobby:

We apologize for stealing your cup cakes.

Little Pete:

We are sorry…we have no excuse to do that…not even if we are hungry; we should have asked asked.

Cut away shots of the other boys watching and laughing…establish a P.O. V shot in one frame.

The lady pays for the cup cakes but the seller rejects the money and hugs the boys.

Cut to:

Scene 23:   mid/cus

Int:

Rita continues to ask question in deep fascination.

Rita:

You may have done some very serious homework to identify all these.

Bobby:

When you love something or someone deeply; you should give it your best attention.

Rita:
And where does that leave me?

Bobby:
Where you are Masheri

Rita:
Which is?

Bobby:
Next to me

Rita:
For ever?

Bobby:
For ever…(gets up)
Let's go to bed

Rita:
Ok…if you say so
(They get up)

Cut to:

NEXT DAY

Scene 24:   Ms/cu shots
Int:
Morning… the studio; A live session, the musicians are practicing a
African Jamaican Culture song; ZION.

Bobby is the lead singer; Sly, Jnr, Rosie and Mercia are
members…they belt Zion.

Song:
His foundation is in the Holy Mountains of Zion
Zion yeahaaaa
The Lord loveth the gate of Zion more than the dwellings of Jacob

Zion yeahaa

Holy Zion,
Holy Holy Zion
Holy Zion,

Holy Holy Zion
Holy Zion,
Holy Holy Zion
Holy Zion,
Holy Holy Zion

Nationality,
No take you to Zion
Passport,
No take you to Zion,
Green Card,
No take you to Zion,
Visa,
No take you to Zion,

Nationality,
No take you to Zion ehee ehee
Passport,
No take you to Zion, ehee
Green Card,
No take you to Zion, ehee ehee
Visa,
No take you to Zion, ehee

Holy Zion,
Holy Holy Zion
Holy Zion,
Holy Holy Zion
Holy Zion,
Holy Holy Zion
Holy Zion,
Holy Holy Zion

Power,
No take you to Zion,
Money,
No take you to Zion,
I yam black

No take I to Zion
You are white
No take you to Zion

Holy Zion,
Holy Holy Zion
Holy Zion,
Holy Holy Zion
Holy Zion,
Holy Holy Zion
Holy Zion,
Holy Holy Zion

Heheheeee,
King of kings
Lord of lords
Conquaring Lion of the tribe of Juda
Power of the Trinity
Light of the world

Shout joyfully
Unto the Most High Jah Rastafari I
All the Earth break forth in song I say

Let the Sea roar
And let all the rivers
Clap their hands joyfully,

I and I God
Conquer Death and Hell
And the gate of Hell cannot prevail

No tell I and I about no semetry,

No tell I and I about no death,
Tell I and I about the Holy Mount Zion,

Where peace and love remain,
Yes sons and daughters

We know

The Most High Jah Rastafari I
Is the ruler of Zion and Earth
Now Rasta you know the truth

Rasta you see the truth
Teach them
Teach them Rasta I say

Holy Zion,
Holy Holy Zion
Holy Zion,
Holy Holy Zion

Nationality,
No take you to Zion
Passport,
No take you to Zion,
Green Card,
No take you to Zion,
Visa,
No take you to Zion,

Power,
No take you to Zion,
Money,
No take you to Zion,
I yam black,
No take I to Zion,
You are white,
No take you to Zion,
Holy Zion,

Holy Holy Zion
Holy Zion,
Holy Holy Zion
Holy Zion,
Holy Holy Zion

Holy Zion,
Holy Holy Zion

Only clean hands
And pure in heart
Shall enter Zion

JAH RASTAFARI

[Guitar Cords; ||: Fm | Bb ES | ES :||]

Slow dissolve to Bob Marley's picture

Feed to black...

Feed in:

Scene 25:   ms / cus
Int/Ext:
Rita and her two friends are at McDonalds eating...her phone rings
and she picks it... looks at the caller identity, smiles.

Rita:
Hi Baby...are you done?

Bobby:
Almost... we're going to the temple though...wanna come with your
friends.

Rita:
No...still busy; you know we're not into that stuff.

Bobby:
It is well…hopefully; you'll find reasons to join me one of these days.

Rita:
Ya Baby…maybe

Bobby:
I promise you…you will

Rita:
Don't hold your breath

Bobby:
I love you…see you later

Rita:
Love you too…bye
(Drops the phone smiling; her friend comments)

Lebo: smiling too
Love birds…**(starts to sing in a mocking fashion)**
I'm in love with a Rastaman.

Rita: tries to hit her mockingly; they laugh
You're full of it

Cut to:

Scene 26:
Ext: ms/ls/sc
Aerial view of Johannesburg, bringing botanical garden part of the Zoo lake.
Enter the sound of music ; "Jah made us!" by African Jamaican Culture

Song:
Hail Jah Rastafari I
Hail Him for food, clothes and shelter,

Hail Him,
For everything which is good,

Hail Jah Rastafari I,
Hail Him,

Hail Him,
Hail Him,

Human your are so blessed,
The earth is the Lord,

And the fullness therein,
It no make sense to trust mankind,

Better trust the Almighty,
I yam living on the mercies of Jah,

And not on the system,
To say mi no fit praise Jah Rastafari I,

Is Jah who made us, you know,
And not we ourselves,

He made the sun,
He made moon,

He made the stars,
He made the earth,

And everything,
That dwell therein,

He is the king of kings,
The Lord of lords,

Conquaring Lion of the tribe of Juda,
Ilect of God,

The earth most rightful ruler,
King Haile Selassie I is the Almighty one,

Everything is equal under the sun,
That is created by Jah,

Guide and protect I and I
Oh Jah Jah,

Through all these stages,
Jah love I

That is why I yam around today,
I love Jah,

That is why I yam around to sing,

Hail Jah Rastafari I,
Hail Him,

Hail Him,
Hail Him,

Hail Jah Rastafari I,
Hail Him,

Hail Him,
Hail Him,

[Guitar Cords; G Am D G F]

A clearing in the middle of woodland by the zoo lake.
Zachy, Bobby, Sly and Tuffy arrive; calls Chief…he emerges from a small hut made from tarpaulin and they greet…

Chief: carrying a small pot with smoke coming from it.
Irie Jah people…peace from the Most
High…Iverliving…Iverfaithful... Iversure King Haile Selassie I

(He brings rolls of herb from a small bag; they greet him and take one after the other)

Tuffy: Takes the spliff as he greets
Greetings brother man

Chief:
Peace
(Moves on to Bobby)

Bobby:
Greetings son of our father King Haile Selassie I
(Takes the spliff)

Chief:
Unity
(Moves to Sly)

Sly: Takes the spliff
Peace, progress in the world Rastaman

Chief:
Brotherhood
(Moves over to Zachy)

Zachy:
Jah love Brother ….one love…together as one.

Bobby:
The great Jah Rastafari prophet Bob Marley once said Emancipation of the Black man is in his hands.

They light up and start to smoke

Cut to:

Scene 27:   estab/mid/cu
Ext:

A Scrap yard; Iceman sits across the counter checking the accounts papers; he is the owner of the Scrap yard and a local car thief who buys stolen vehicles, rebuilds and sells. His two assistants are there; doubling as thugs and personal bodyguards…

Iceman: talks to Fats
Fats…is the car here?

Fats:
Last night Mr. Ice

Iceman:
Call Zachy then

Fats:
Yes Bossman… **(Calls Tiny)**
Tiny, call Rastaman, tell him the baby is here.

Iceman:
When are the goods arriving?

Fats:
Next tomorrow Mr. Ice

Iceman:
And my money

Fats:
On its way already

Two (2) girls walk in; one begins to greet.

Jelly:
Hi people…my Ice

Iceman: Looks up
Now these are my Jelly and Lollipop

(Beckons on them to come to him)
Now…come to Daddy
(They go to him; he hugs them)

Lollipop:
What's the deal Fatsy?

Fats:
The baby goes tonight…have a new order

Jelly:
Cool…we'll get down on it

Iceman: smiles pleasantly
Now why won't I smile all the time?

Lollipop:
Your wish is our command…Iceman

Cut to:

Scene 28: Ms/mid/cu
Ext:
The shrine…Zachy and the men are busy smoking their lives out.
Chief is busy with the supplies and they live in their self-made
world…they discuss police actions as it concerns them.

Chief: throws them a newspaper
Our friends destroyed Pigs peak yesterday.

Zachy: shocked to hear that; picks the paper.
What? …how?...when?

Tuffy:
Holy shit

Bobby:
The best skank…Yo! Man…man…man

Sly:
That was a disaster meen!...Swazi gold is the ultimate.

Chief:
I heard they're coming for us

Bobby:
What?...what are we gonna do?

Chief:
They'll see no shit man

Tuffy:
Chief ooo; you're the man

Chief:
Believe

Zachy:
That's why we're here
(His phone rings; he picks it)

SPLIT SCREEN

Scene 29:   mid/cu
Ext/int:
Tiny is on the line; he informs him his car is ready and Iceman wants
to see him; he jumps up and throws a joyful punch in the air.

Zachy:
Irie...Zachy here. How may I help you?

Fats:
Hei Zachy boy...its Fats

Zachy:
Hei..Fatso...what's up my man?

Fats:
The Baby is sorted…Bossman wants you to come in later…

Zachy: shouts for joy; throwing punches in the air.
Later…I'm coming straight away; can't wait my man.
(Drops the phone; tells everybody)

men…men…men, my car is ready

They celebrate…

Cut to:

Scene 30:   Ms/mid/cus
Int:
The studio…recording is in session; Bobby is recording a song.
Carry on Rastaman and Rastawoman.

Bobby: sings
Oppression is so strong
Ina Babylon
Sufferation is so strong
Ina Babylon
Temptation is so strong
Ina Babylon
Wickedness is so strong
Ina Babylon

Nevertheless carry on
Rastaman carry on
Carry on Rastaman carry on
Carry on Rastaman carry on
Carry on Rastaman carry on

Carry on Pretty Rastawoman carry on
Carry on Pretty Rastawoman carry on
Carry on Pretty Rastawoman carry on
Carry on Pretty Rastawoman carry on

In a Jah Jah own way
In a Jah Jah own way
Persecution we must bear
Trial and crosses in our way
Including what the Policemen do
The hotter the battle the sweeter Jah Jah intervene

Carry on Rastaman carry on
Carry on Rastaman carry on
Carry on Rastaman carry on
Carry on Rastaman carry on

Carry on Pretty Rastawoman carry on
Carry on Pretty Rastawoman carry on
Carry on Pretty Rastawoman carry on
Carry on Pretty Rastawoman carry on

In a Jah Jah own way
In a Jah Jah own way
Persecution we must bear
Trial and crosses in our way
Including what the Policemen do
The hotter the battle the sweeter Jah Jah intervene
Carry on as you can remember
Straight is the road that leads to destruction
The road to righteousness is narrow O

Carry on Rastaman carry on
Carry on Rastaman carry on
Carry on Rastaman carry on
Carry on Rastaman carry on

Carry on Pretty Rastawoman carry on
Carry on Pretty Rastawoman carry on
Carry on Pretty Rastawoman carry on
Carry on Pretty Rastawoman carry on

In a Jah Jah own way
In a Jah Jah own way

Persecution we must bear
Trial and crosses in our way
Including what the Policemen do
The hotter the battle the sweeter Jah Jah intervene
Carry on as you can remember
Straight is the road that leads to destruction

The road to righteousness is narrow O

Carry on Rastaman carry on
Carry on Rastaman carry on
Carry on Rastaman carry on
Carry on Rastaman carry on

Carry on Pretty Rastawoman carry on
Carry on Pretty Rastawoman carry on
Carry on Pretty Rastawoman carry on
Carry on Pretty Rastawoman carry on

In a Jah Jah own way
In a Jah Jah own way
Persecution we must bear
Trial and crosses in our way
Including what the Policemen do
The hotter the battle the sweeter Jah Jah intervene
Carry on as you can remember
Straight is the road that leads to destruction
The road to righteousness is narrow O

Carry on

[Guitar Cords; ||: G | F :||]

Slow fade

Street shot

Scene 31: creative shots
Ext:

A busy street;

The music is heard above the noise of street ambience.

One in a row of slow moving cars, Zachy is driving a quality car, playing same music.

He drives up the street, turns into an intersection; stops at a robot; he continues.

Feed in

Scene 32: Ms/mid
Int:
Back at the studio, they are still in session. Zachy walks in…invites them to come and see his new car; they follow.

Create studio ambience

Zachy: walks in
Men…men…men; my baby is here; want to come see?

Sly: stops working at the CONSOLE… signals Bobby in the singing booth, he comes out; they follow Zachy to see the car.

Cut to:

LATER THAT EVENING

Scene 33: Ms/mid/cu
Int:
Bobby is in the house with Rita; they talk.

Rita: Very close to him

How was your day?

Bobby:
Busy…busy…busy.

Rita:
Doing?

Bobby:
What do one do in the studio?
Recording.

Rita:
Whole day?

Bobby:
Almost…we went to the temple too

Rita:
Where is that one?... the joint?

Bobby:
Ya… Zachy bought a new car

Rita:
And where did the money come from?

Bobby:
Is that what you ask a man?

Rita:
I didn't know he does any other job…anyway; tell me more about Bob Marley and why you love him so much.

Bobby:
Simple…my life was like it was carved out from his.

He never knew his father well…just like me. You know; one of those useless Dads who has little regard for their off springs.

Rita: touched
Shame…yet

Bobby: interrupts
He grew in a very violent and crime riddled environment just like here

Quick dissolve

Scene 34:   Crane/Ms/ special cuts
Ext:
Scenario 1
A lazy street; Two (2) gun trotting girls; Jelly and Lollipop points a gun at a man at a robot; rob him of his car and drives off in it.
The girls walk down the street fearlessly…they are wearing balaclavas, Jelly gets to a man in his car at a robot intersection kicks his car pretending to get hurt, the man notices her , asks what's the problem…Lollipop points a gun at him and orders him to put both hands on his head and get out of the car.. He looks at her, she quickly corks the gun; the man gets out and begins to run.

The girls jump into the car and screeches off…

Quick deep to black as we hear the sound of police sirens...
Then voices over a police two-way- radio.

Cut to:

Scene 35: ls/mid/cus
Ext:
Scenario 2

Two (2) boys and a girl with tattoos and scarf chase down another man down the street and shot him dead; then runs away.

The man being chased is running frantically; jumps across a picket fence and falls. He runs into a street park and continues running looking back in deep fear…they continue chasing him.

He runs in front of a deserted street and is tripped by something, he falls…

The first boy gets to him, points a gun at him while he is on the ground; he raises both hands looking at him and pleading for his life…

The other boy and girl gets to him…the girl shoots him without blinking and they walk slowly away.

Cut to:

Scene 36: ls/mid/sc
Ext:
Scenario 3
A police van blaring siren speeds down a busy street chasing after a run-away car.

A street car chase…a drunken man driven dangerously along the road; he is chased by the Metro police in a wild chase until he surrenders…they orders him out of the car with his hands over his head. They gave him breathalyzer test; handcuffs him and puts him in their car. Then they drive away.

Deep to black…
We hear the sound of human voices
Opens up to a road-side church laden with people…

Scene 37: ms/ls/mids
Ext:
Scenario 4:
A false preacher preaches immorality and wealth at all cost; the people give him money. He professes to see the future and tells the people what they want to hear…
Lines Impro…

Focus on performance

The few congregation chants, claps and sings wildly as the preacher urges them to seek the address and e-mail of God telling them that God is only a click away…he can help them seek God on Facebook and twitter.

Deep to black

Scene 38: ls/mid/cus
Ext:
Scenario 5
A roadside park; the men are busy smoking herb; the police arrives; arrests all of them.

Quick feed in

Scene 39:
Int:

Back at Bobby's flat; he continues to narrate the story to her drawing comparison with his own life. In the face of all these challenges; he never forgot his guitar or his songs.

Enter music and/or video of Bobby singing… "The Mud House" by African Jamaican Culture

Song:
Do you remember
How we lived our life
In the mud house?

Usually,

Do you remember
How we lived our life

In the mud house?

Do you remember
How we lived our life
In the mud house?

Usually,

Do you remember
How we lived our life
In the mud house?

Rats lived with us,
Snakes lived with us,
Birds lived with us,
Lizards lived with us,
Wall Geckos
Lived with us too,

Do you remember
How we lived our life
In the mud house?

Usually,

Do you remember
How we lived our life
In the mud house?

Do you remember
How we lived our life
In the mud house?

Usually,

Do you remember
How we lived our life
In the mud house?

Snakes wriggled upon us,
Rats chop-up our heels, yeah
Millipedes walked upon us too,

Do you remember?

Do you remember

How we lived our life
In the mud house?

Usually,

Do you remember,
How we lived our life,
In the mud house,

Do you remember
How we lived our life
In the mud house?

Usually,

Do you remember
How we lived our life
In the mud house?

Ants bite us,
Mosquitoes bite us,
Rain drops on us,

Through the leaking roof, oh yeah,

Do you remember
How we lived our life
In the mud house?

Usually,

Do you remember
How we lived our life
In the mud house?
Do you remember
How we lived our life
In the mud house?

Usually,

Do you remember
How we lived our life
In the mud house?

The road I travel,
I never forget,
The travelling souls,
Sing with the birds
Cats fight in the night,
Do you remember?

Brothers and Sisters,
Never give up,
Because, the biggest man,
You ever did see,
Was once just a baby,
Do you remember? Do you remember?

When we usually go to haunt for Locusts,
Grasshoppers and Termites,
For Mama to make soup,
Do you remember?

You should remember,
Try to remember,

Do you remember
How we lived our life
In the mud house?

Usually,

Do you remember
How we lived our life
In the mud house?

Do you remember
How we lived our life
In the mud house?

Usually,

Do you remember
How we lived our life
In the mud house?

Do you remember
How we lived our life
In the mud house?

Usually,

Do you remember
How we lived our life
In the mud house?

Do you remember
How we lived our life
In the mud house?

Usually,

Do you remember
How we lived our life
In the mud house?

[Guitar Cords; :| Gm Gm | F F |:]

Slow fade
Scene 40:   ls/mids/cus
Int:
Back at Bobby's; Rita comments

Rita:
One thing I like about the man is that he was extremely talented.

Bobby:
No…Masheri…he was beyond that; he was talent himself; he was immortal and he said so himself.

Rita:
What did he say?

Bobby:
That the world will never forget him

Cut to:

Scene 41:
Int/Ext:
Scrap yard; Iceman inspects the car Jelly and Lollipop brought smiling from cheek to cheek; they're all drinking hot drinks…he finishes inspection and orders his boys to pieces it and switch the parts.

Iceman: hugs the girls
What can we do without us?

They all start laughing

Iceman:
Let's go out there and make millions…the world is a shit place

Fats:
Man no die no rotten

Iceman:
Say it again; this one goes to Tanzania; we've got jobs for Maputo, Luanda and Bulawayo.

Jelly:
Give us the shit; we do the shit.

Lollipop:
That's the way it is

Tiny hands a piece of paper over to Jelly; she looks at it, smiles and gives it to Lollipop.

They hug Iceman

Iceman:
Let's meet in my house tonight

Jelly:
Cool lover boy

Lollipop:
We see you people later

Fats: crosses his finger
Fingers crossed

Cut to:

Scene 42:   estb/mid/cu
Ext:

The band is in practice; all band members are there except Bobby; they sit and smoke herb waiting for him and discussing Zachy's car and other things.

Zachy:
I wonder what is holding Bobby; his phone is off.

Sly:
I'm sure he'll be here soonest.

Mercia: suggests
Let's do spliff while we wait

Rosey:
Not a bad idea

Sly:
Zachy meen!...that your car is a bomb. I hope it's not hot

Zachy:
Why should it be?

Sly:
Just asking…you know; Iceman is many things.

Mercia:
This spliff is not as good.

Tuffy:
Or maybe we need to have our own farm.

Rosie:
Farm…where?

Tuffy: (Points up)

Up there in the mountain; away from the eyes of these stupid cops.

Sly:
Those people are everywhere

Cut to:

Scene 43:
Ext: ms/mid

Bobby and Rita are walking towards the studio, hand-in-hand. Bobby is trying to convince her to come and watch them play...
She is not fully interested but only want to please him.

Bobby:
Tell you what; if you don't love what you'll see, I'll make you dinner for three nights ok...

Rita: laughs mockingly
You...make dinner; Jesus is coming

Bobby:
I promise you

Rita:
You I'm not really cut out for this; but...you're the boss

Bobby:
And you're the Boss lady
(They turn a corner)
Feed to black

Scene 44:   Ms./mid/cus
Int:
Bobby and Rita join the others in the studio... They embrace each other; welcome Rita, then start to practice.

Zachy:

Waoh!...are we safe today
(Goes and hugs Rita)
With your presence in our midst

Rita:
Everyone is completely safe and at home. I came to enjoy myself.

Sly:
And that you will do…we promise.

Mercia:
You can even join us for more fun.

Rita:
No…thanks. Singing is not my strong point at all.

Rosey:
No one started out perfect…

Rita:
No people…I'd rather watch you people; even if for today; maybe
next time.

Bobby:
If there will ever be a next time; I knew what it took me to bring her
here.
(They start laughing)

**They start practicing, playing African Jamaican Culture's song,
Mosiah Marcus Garvey/Africans Unite.**

The Jamaican Hero
Mosiah Marcus Garvey
Born as another Moses
Come to lead I and I Africans
To a spiritual victory
To overcome our mental slavery

The Prophet of African Integrity
He fight for the unification of Africans
The U.N.I.A [Universal Negro Improvement Association]
Six Million Strong Song
Africa's New Redemption Song

Africans Unite
Africans Unite
Africans Unite
Africans Unite

The Prophet of African Integrity
He fight for the unification of Africans
The U.N.I.A [Universal Negro Improvement Association]
Six Million Strong Song
Africa's New Redemption Song

Africans Unite
Africans Unite
Africans Unite
Africans Unite

(Guitar Cords; G | A-)

Cut to:

Scene 45: ms/mid/cus
Int:
Bobby's flat…he is with Rita and they discuss her interest in the band, wanting to know more about Bob Marley.

Rita: cutting apple and talking to Bobby;
I am really impressed with your dedication to your music thing. This Bob Marley man must be truly great.

Bobby:
Ya…for me personally, it is human aspect of who he is/was that inspires me in everything I do.

Rita:
How do you mean?

Bobby:
His rag to riches story; the fact that he was a nobody; born by a non-de script father who never stayed with him or his mother and a teenage mother with nothing but hope to live for.

Rita:
Waoh! …That is truly inspirational. Knowing that greatness is truly a seed of a profound thought groomed within a healthy mind.

Bobby: Thoughtful
The triumph of the human spirit…I use the circumstances of our own lives to measure the size of his heart.

Rita:
What do you mean?

Bobby:
Just take a look around you…violence, crime, bigotry, drugs, destroyed values…you know, lives laid to waste.

Quick fade to flash…flashbacks.

Scene 46:
Ext: slomo…
A lazy street, a group of boys and girls; most of them carrying guns; they walk in huge gaits as if going for a fight with another group.
They hear the sound of police siren and disappears into an adjoining building.

They appear on the next street; meet another group who blocks their way and threatens a fight…they retreat.

Fade to flash

Scene 47:
Ext: ls/mid/sc
Next day…mid day.

A street park; Little Bobby and friends are playing soccer; the ball lands in front of one amongst a group of bigger boys walking by; one of them seizes the ball.

Little Bobby goes and demands for the ball; the boy refuses to release it.

Little Bobby:
Give me my ball

Big boy: makes as if to slap him

Get the fuck out of my face…little swag.

Little Bobby:
Don't call me names
(Kicks him on the heel). Give me my ball
The big boy slaps him on the head.

Big boy:
I'll kill you motherfucker
Shoves him aside

Little Bobby: shouts at him while his friends watch.

A bigger boy instructs the boy to release the ball; he does as told and throws the ball away.

Little Bobby picks the ball and they continued to play.

Fade to flash

Scene 48:

Ext: ms/mid/sc

Another part of town…slow moving vehicles. A group of school children in uniform walks along the road. Other children throw pebbles at them from a higher embankment.

The kids notice where the pebbles are coming from…run towards them.

Cut to:

Scene 49:
Int: ms/mid/sc
Bobby's flat…he is with Rita, they continue to discuss Bob Marley.

Rita:
Ya ne? …Poverty is bad eh? It goes hand in hand with crime.

Bobby:
It is a sin…I will never be poor; **(Touches her by the shoulder)** We will never be poor…life is what you make of it.

Rita:
It's all about commitment and dedication to what one does.

Bobby:
And belief in one self no matter the odds or how and what the people say about you.

Rita:
So long as we are focused on our desire for greatness and not compromise it with undue decisions.

Bobby:
The highest quality a man could have is unshakable strength to face all odds and succeed without resorting to crime and criminality.

Rita:
I agree…obviously supported by a strong woman who lays down the law and make you follow…what about Bob Marley?

Bobby:
He married Rita

Rita:
Rita…you joking right?

Bobby:
Nope… he fell in love with a Rastafarian woman who converted him
to Rastafarian

Rita:
What is Rastafarian?

Bobby:
It is a way of life; culture; development of reggae; historical
relevance.

Rita:
Now, you've confused me all the more.

Bobby:
Ok Masheri…I am a Rastafarian and you'll learn more as we go on.

Rita:
And Rita?

Bobby:
She is the love of his life, they were together in the face of all
challenges…
…That was before he moved to America to live with his mother.

Cut to:

Scene 50:
Ext: ls/ms/mid/sc
A clearing within a park overlooking the city; the boys are there
smoking spliff and talking…a phone call comes to Zachy and he quickly.

Zachy:
This girl is really into Bobby; he hardly has time for us as much.

Mercia:
What do you expect...the girl is good

Rosie:
Yeah...I agree; she makes him shine

Sly:
But she's not a Rastafarian

Tuffy:
That's the problem...he needs a disciple

Zachy's phone rings...he picks and checks caller ID; sits up immediately.

Zachy:
Iric Iceman

v/o:
Come to my shop now.

Zachy:
Everything good?

Iceman:
Come as quickly as you can...alright?

Zachy:
I'm there
(Gets up)
Men let me see Iceman...be back now.

Cut to:

Scene 51:
Int: ms/mid/cu
Bobby's flat; Rita and Bobby continue.

Rita:
What happened in America?

Bobby:
He went to see his mother…actually lived with her for a while but the call of music brought him back to Jamaica.

Rita:
How did he go from poverty to a global super star?

Bobby:
It is a lesson in the triumph of the human spirit and greatness of God.

Rita:
Tell me more about this man; his story sounds intriguing.

Bobby:
Where do I start? …How do I begin, there is so much to tell and huge lessons to be learnt.

Rita:
Start again from the beginning.

Bobby:
That is a huge task

Rita:
Go on…let's test your knowledge of him unless your claims are fake.

Bobby:
How can you say that?

Rita:
Prove yourself then; from the beginning to the end.

Bobby:
By that you mean?

Rita:
From birth to death.

Bobby:
Ok...wipe your ears; open your mind...enjoy the ride.

Cut:

Scene 52:
Back at the scrap yard
Int / Ext: ms/mid/cus
Zachy enters to meet Iceman; Fats meet him at the door; he takes him into the office to see Iceman.

Zachy:
Hei Boss

Iceman:
How are you doing?

Zachy:
Not too badly...still battling with the band.

Iceman: passive
I see...where is my money?

Zachy: taken by surprise
Oh...that one, it will be ready in three (3) days. It is sent already; just waiting to clear.

Iceman: stands up and goes near to him
Are you sure of that?

Zachy:
Come on Boss...what's my name?

Iceman: looks at him as if weighing him up, pats him on the back.
I believe you...you know how it is?

Zachy:
Ya...no stories

Iceman: pats him on the back again
No stories my friend.
(Begins to go)
Come...your order is here; come check it out
(They go out to the scrap yard)

Cut to:

Scene 53:
Ext: ms/mid/sc
Rooftop of a building; Bobby is with Rita. He has his guitar; he plays it gently while they talk.

Bobby:

We've discussed his birth before but since you want a new start.

Rita:
Yes my love…I really want to know

Bobby:
Ok…here we go;

Deep to black

Voice over

Robert Nesta Marley the legendary 'King of Reggae' was born on the 6th of February 1945 in Nine Mile, Saint Ann, Jamaica. His father, Norval Marley was a Jamaican of English descent while his teenage mother was a local black woman, Cedella Booker.

Rita:
Teenage mother?

Bobby:
Ya…

Rita:
I think they were not married.

Bobby:
Yes…but they planned to do that.

Rita:
And what stopped them.

Bobby:
Norval left Kingston before that and never returned until he died in 1955; he saw his son only once in his lifetime.

Rita:
What a shame

Cut to:

Scene 54:
Int: ms/mid/sc
Studio… the band is rehearsing; they play **African Jamaican Culture's song; "Jah Call All"**

Jah call all
To repentance

Jah call all
To repentance
Jah call all
To repentance
Jah call all
To repentance

You searching You searching
You searching
You searching You searching
You searching
And you searching You searching
You searching

I see you searching for freedom

I see you want freedom
I see you want peace
Love
And happiness
To enjoy peace
Love

And happiness
My beloved brothers and sisters
The Almighty God of Isreal
Jah Rastafari
Will have to forgive you
For all the wrongs
You've been doing

Jah Rastafari is the only way
My friend
So make refuge in Him
Before its too late
For He is coming
Soon
Or very soon
To judge the Earth

With righteousness
Shall He judge the World
And the peoples
That dwell therein

With equity
With equity
With equity
With equity

Jah call all
To repentance
Jah call all
To repentance
Jah call all
To repentance
Jah call all

To repentance

Lightning

Thunder
Brimstone
Earthquake
Blood
And fire
Roll River Jordan roll (Jordan River)

Behold He that keepeth I and I
Shall not slumber
Behold He that keepeth Isreal
Shall not slumber nor sleep
Behold He that keepeth
A resting place for I and I
Over the Hills
And across the Valley
Behold I see you've been

Searching
Searching
Searching
Searching
For freedom
I see you want freedom
I see you want peace
Love
And happiness
To enjoy peace
Love
And happiness
My beloved brothers and sisters
The Almighty God of Isreal
Jah Rastafari
Will have to forgive you
For all the wrongs
You've been doing

Jah Rastafari is the only way
My friend

So make refuge in Him
Before its too late
For He is coming
Soon
Or very soon
To judge the Earth
With righteousness

Shall He judge the World
And the peoples that dwell therein

With equity
With equity
With equity
With equity

Jah call all
To repentance

Jah call all
To repentance
Jah call all
To repentance
Jah call all
To repentance

[Guitar Cords; D | C]

Cut to:

Scene 55:
Ext: ls/mid/sc
Another part of town; fairly busy street; Zachy is cruising in the new
car supplied him by Iceman.
Bob Marley blasts from the sound system.
He comes to an intersection, stops and waits for a red robot to change
to green.

Sees someone he knows in walking down the road; waves and they greet…drives off…

Scene 56:
Int/Ext: ms/mid/sc
The Scrap yard; Lollipop and Jelly drive in to meet Iceman; they discuss money and strategies.

They drive in; Lollipop comes out first; Jelly follows behind.
Gets to his office; talking excitedly… opens the door, words dries up in her mouth as they see Iceman smooching a big breasted girl. He notices them and stops; the girl pulls her clothes down. Lolli turns and runs away…

Jelly goes after her.
Lolli wait…Lolli; come on girl, wait.
Lollipop stops by a distance…she gets to her.
P.O.V shot favoring all in one frame;
What are you doing girl?... is this you?...when did it all start?

Lollipop: apologizes
I'm sorry…it's just that it is so wrong.

Jelly: whispers in her ear.
There will be time for a pound of flesh.

The girl is smiling; Iceman notices and shouts at her…

Iceman: angrily
What are you smiling at Bitch
(Shoves her away)
get your big fat everything out of here now.
she looks at him in anger and walks away slowly and seductively.
Iceman slumps into the chair. Lolli and Jelly walks back to him.

Lolli: gives a half baked apology
I apologize Ice; that was immature of me.

Iceman: Looks up at them
I understand; you know, I seldom say these words...**(still looking at them)**...I am sorry, deeply sorry; it was immature and callous of me to behave in this manner.

Jelly:
Yes...it just did not roll.

Iceman: tries to cheer them up
Come on now ladies...

Quick cut:

Scene 57:
Ext/Int: ls/mid/sc
Downtown, another part of town; Zachy drives into a building parking bay; gets out of the car and walks to the lift; enters and the lift goes. Camera shows floor number as the lift stops and he comes out.
He enters the studio in excitement and invites his colleagues to come and check out his new car; they follow him to the parking bay.

Dialogue impro.
Cut to:

Scene 58:
Int: ms/mid/sc
Back at the scrap yard...

Iceman: to Lolli
I didn't mean to hurt you Lol.
(Goes to her; tries to hold her, she evades his hug)

Lolli: apologizes
I'm sorry as well… I didn't know what came over me.

Iceman: orders her to come to him
Come here my Baby…come

(Opens his arms for a hug; she walks into it, he hugs her)
it will never happen again I promise you. Not in this lifetime.

Lolli:
Never in this lifetime because I am carrying your baby.

(Both Iceman and Jelly shout in shock surprise)

Quick cut:

Scene 59:
Int: ms/mid/sc
Bobby's flat…he is lying on the carpeted floor; Rita lies next to him…they smooch and cuddle and talk about Bob Marley.

Bobby:
Life in Trench town was hard to say the least. Poverty stinks you know; it demeans us as human beings and denies us so much.

Rita:
Now you talk like a Priest

(They laugh)

Bobby:
Maybe it's because I know it first hand. It presents us with huge challenges but he was equal to it, thanks to two things.

Rita:

Things like what and what?

Bobby:
First he was naturally strong and was able to fight his way out of adverse situations and impose his personality on them.
Secondly, he was too talented and utilized both gifts well as life went on.

Rita:
You knew him too well.

Bobby:
I had no choice but to get to know him. You know; he was too strong that they named him TUFF GONG despite his body build.

Rita:
How do you mean Body build.

Bobby:
He wasn't a giant and yet he was able to dismantle them…he often fought his way out of situations physically; he also loved soccer too and played it a great deal

Cut to:

LATER THAT NIGHT

Scene 60:
Ext/int: ls/mid/sc
Another part of town…
Iceman's house in an exclusive suburb. Iceman and Lolli are in bed, they discuss events that occurred earlier in the day.

Iceman:
Baby, this baby thing; were you joking or trying to pull my legs.

Lolli:
No one jokes with babies.

Iceman:
When did you notice that?

Lolli:
Two weeks ago

Iceman:
And you kept it from me?

Lolli:
I needed to be sure

Iceman:
And you're sure now?

Lolli:
100%

Cut to:

Scene 61: ls/mid/sc
Another part of town; Bobby's flat
Int:
Bobby and Rita continues

Rita:
Where was his wife when he went to live in America?

Bobby:
In Jamaica, he didn't stay too long though, he came back to Jamaica and that was where his music career took off.

Rita:
How?

Bobby:
He met and teamed up with Peter Tosh and Bunny Livingston to form a group called "The Wailers" that was even before he married his wife; when he came back, the group became stronger.

Rita:
Wow!

Bobby:
Ya...Infact they collaborated with Lee Scratch Perry to release some of their earliest and finest tracks like "Soul Rebel", "400 years", "Small Axe"...

Rita:
Yo!...you know it all

Bobby:
To me he remains the greatest influence in everything I do

Cut to:

Scene 62:
Int: est/ms/mid/sc
Another part of town; Iceman's house...he continues his dialogue with Lolli.

Iceman:
What do you intend to do about it?

Lolli:
What do you mean?

Iceman:
You know what I mean; how are you going to manage a baby and our job?

Lolli:
We shall see

Iceman:
Meaning you're keeping the baby

Lolli:
Don't even go there

Iceman: sits up

Baby…we still have Luanda, Maputo and Bulawayo to do and many others that will come.

Lolli:
I know
(Sits up too)
I know the demands and challenges but we shall find a way around it.

Iceman:
Too dangerous

Deep to black

NEXT DAY

Scene 63:
Ext: ls/ms/sc
Another part of town; Zachy is driving on a street, playing music in a cute car. His phone rings, he answers and is talking while driving; A traffic policeman spots him, then follows him.

He stops him and begins to check his license and car papers. Discovers something and calls the office with his two-way radio.

Another cop joins him, they arrest him and drives away with him; a truck comes and tows the car away.

Cut to:

Ext: ms/ls/sc
Scene 64:
… MIX WITH A TOWNSHIP STREET; ROAD SIDE CAR WASH. A MUSIC BOX LAID IN A CORNER BLASTING LOCAL MUSIC.
Two (2) men are there, one is sitting on a broken couch, the other is busy washing different cars; they sing and dance to the music in absolute enjoyment…

A sleek car drives into the car wash; the men rush to it admiring and dancing around it.

The driver comes out; also sleekly dressed, they bow before him selling their handiwork.

Dialogue impro.

Dissolve to:

INTERVAL…INTERVAL…INTERVAL

A Real View of
Bob Marley
through Inspiration 2
THE SAGA CONTINUES

****

Scene 65:
Ext: Ms/mid/sc
Same Loc.
The men are busy washing the car; the owner sits, reading newspaper. Lolli and Jelly drives in; packs next to the car. Jelly checks out the car and praises it. She engages the owner while Lolli talks to the boys to clean their own car.
Jelly sits next to the man, they shake hands.

Jelly: Talks to the man
Hi…I believe that's your car
(Extends her hand for a shake; he shakes her hand; asks her to sit next to him)
Sandra

Clive:
Clive…is that your own car

Sandra:
No, my friend's…mine is a little bit poorer

Clive:

I don't think so…not with the way you look

Sandra:
How do I look?

Clive:
Exquisite; extremely beautiful, gorgeous.

Sandra:
I get it…you're as sleek as your car
(They begin to laugh; Lolli joins them)
Chomi, this man is as sleek as his car.

Lolli: stands next to them
What has he done?
(Extends her hand to Clive)
Hi… Mabel

Clive: stands up; offers her his seat.
Please sit

Lolli:
Are you for real?

Jelly:
See what I said

Lolli: Talks to him
Can I have your number?

Clive:
Ofcourse…I hope I can get yours too

Jelly:
What about me?

Lolli:
Too late
(They start to laugh; share numbers)

Cut to:

Scene 66:
Int: ms/mid/sc
Bobby and Rita are having breakfast and talking about Bob Marley.

They are in the kitchen making Ackee and Bean Curd together. Rita is cooking, bobby is standing next to her.

Rita:
Tell me more about Bob Marley

Bobby:
Aren't you becoming obsessed too?

Rita:
The story is inspiring…I'm really loving it…please tell me more.

Bobby:
Perry sold their records in England without their consent and the collaboration ended; they however started making hits upon hits in the years that followed.

Rita:
Hits like what and what?

Bobby:
Their first album was "Catch a Fire", then "Burning", "Get up stand up", "I shot the Sheriff". They rolled on till 1974 when Peter Tosh and Livingston left to start their own solo careers.

Rita:
Yo!...what a shame; what happened to him after that?

Bobby:
He got even stronger; formed Bob Marley and the Wailers enlisting his wife and two (2) other ladies as his back up singers called the I-Threes.

Rita:
Waoh!... what a story.

Bobby:
They went on a huge run of success with hits like "Natty Dread", "Rastaman Vibration" and others until 1976 when there was an attempt on his life.

Rita:
What!...what happened?

His phone rings...he answers; shocked.

Bobby:
Zachy has been arrested... I need to get to the police station now.

Rita:
What happened'?

Bobby:
Something to do with a stolen car...I'll call you.
(Leaves quickly).

Cut to:

Scene 67:
Int: ls/ms/mid/sc
Police station; police business as usual.
Police holding cell...Zachy sits in a corner, hands holding the jaw.

Deep to black

Scene 68:
Ext: ls/mid/sc

Street leading to the police station. Bobby drops off a meter taxi, walks into the station…

Deep to Black

Scene 69:
Int: ls/sc
Police front counter…Bobby walks in and looks around. Goes to a lady policewoman on an end of the counter.
Camera on a wide shot…

He enquires about Zachy…waits; the lady walks away…

She comes back; points to him where to go and how to get there.

He goes…

M.O.D

Deep to Black

Scene 70:
Ext: ms/mid/sc
Petrol garage, Clive drives in and packs; looks at his watch and sits in the car.

His phone rings, he answers…

Quick cut to:

Scene 71:
Ext: ls/ms/mid/sc
A busy street, Lolli and Jelly are in a car, Jelly is on the phone to Clive.

Jelly:

Please we'll be there in 5 minutes ok?

v/o:
Not a problem… I'll wait

Jelly:
Thanks Babes…see you now.

Lolli:
Shame … he seem a nice man

Jelly:
Ya…but we want the car; no harm intended…just business.

Lolli:
Ya…we'll take him on a ride

Jelly:
That's it…ride of his life

Cut to:

Scene 72:
Int: ms/mid/sc
Back at the police station; holding cell. Bobby is with Zachy,
separated by a bar.

Zachy:
Please you need to get to Iceman quickly…tell him I'm here because
of the car.

Bobby:
Which car?

Zachy:
The Mayback …he knows. Tell him his boys didn't do a good job and
the car is still very hot. Tell him I need his help immediately.

Bobby: (exclaims)

Yo! Bro…what have you gotten yourself into?

Zachy:
Say it again…quick bucks.

Cut to:

Scene 73:

Ext: ls/mid/sc
Lolii and Jelly arrive at the garage; see where Clive parked. Jelly gets out and goes to him… They confer.

Clive gets out of the car; they hug and goes to Lolli; he bends down and gives her a peck on the cheek.

Jelly:
We're on our way to Kasi to see my mother; she's not feeling well, wanna come with?

Clive:
Not a problem; I've got time to spend…can as well spend it with you girls.

Lolli:
Shame…thanks for the compliment; you are hot too Brother.

Jelly:
I agree; may we use your car?
(looks at him seductively)
just to have a feel of it…I love power cars.

Clive:
Sure…you don't have to apologize… we can go if you're ready.

(They leave together to his car).

Cut to:

Scene 74:
Int: ms/mid/sc
Another part of town…
Long shot of the street where the scrap yard is. A taxi pulls in front of it; Bobby gets out of it and walks into the scrap yard.

Cut to:

Scene 75:
Ext:ls/mid/sc
Freeway; Clive is driving with Lolli and Jelly. Jelly is sitting in front with him while Lolli is at the back.

Suddenly, Jelly asks him to stop the car to allow her ease herself.

Clive:
Anything wrong?

Jelly:
I'm sorry I had to do this…I'm really pressed and can't hold it anymore.

Clive:
Sorry about that
(Stops)

Jelly: asks him to join her stating she's afraid walking into the bushes alone.
Please give me a company; can't get into the bushes alone. Lolli can look after your car.

Lolli:
Are you sure of that?

Jelly:
I trust him

Clive: confused, follows her
If you say so

They walk into the bushes

Cut to:

Scene 76:
Int: ms/mid/sc
Scrap yard; Bobby walks in…greets and requests to see Iceman.

Bobby:
Good day people.

Fats:
Ola! …how can we help you

Bobby:
I came to see Iceman with a message from Zachy.

Fats:
Iceman …what message?

Bobby:
I'd rather talk to Iceman if you don't mind.

Fats:
Sorry Boss…you need to talk to me first; that's the protocol.

Tiny: Talks to him from across the desk
Talk to him Bro. or else there is nothing we can do.

Bobby: Looks at them; then talks
He said he should come to help him out.

Tiny:
What happened?

Bobby:
He was arrested by the police for the car.

Fats:
Which car?

Bobby:
He said it's the Mayback.

They look at each other.

Fats:
Which police station?

Bobby:
Jeppe

They look at each other again.

Tiny:
Alright…go, tell him the Boss is not here but we'll come shortly.

Bobby:
Ok…thanks

(He leaves)

Lolli: leans forward as if wanting to talk into his ear and points a gun to his neck.

Cut to:

Scene 77:
Ext: ms/mid/sc
Inside the bushes by the freeway; Jelly is under a small tree fiddling with her cloth; suddenly she pulls a gun…asks Clive to undress.

Clive: in deep shock, begins to undress
What's going on?

Jelly:
No question you fool…remove your cloth…everything.

Clive: angry
Why are you doing this?

Jelly:
If you don't shut up; I'll leave you completely nude. Be a good man and you'll have your pants

Lolli joins them…goes straight to him and handcuffs his right hand to a thick shrub and forces him to kneel down.
They drop the cuff key and clothes a distance from him and leave with the car key.

Jelly:
Nice doing business with you.

Lolli:
You're a nice man Clive; it's just that girls gotta do what girls gotta do.
Sorry.

They leave; he begins to walk on his knees to where the cloth and key is.

Cut to:

Scene 78:
A Street in Braamfontein
Int: ls/mid/sc
Rita is with her two (2) friends, Lebo and Tina; she phones Bobby to find out what's going on.

Rita: dials his number... he answers

v/o:
Hello

Rita:
Babes how far?

v/o:
I'm almost done. I'll be home in 10 minutes.

Rita:
Ok...I'm out with Lebs and Tina but I'll see you then.

v/o:
Cool...love you

Rita:
Love you too.
Drops the line.

Lebo:
What happened?

Rita:
He went to help Zachy sort out some police issue.

Tina:
Marijuana?

Rita:
I don't know

Cut to:

Scene 79:
Ext/Int: ms/mid/sc
Scrap yard
Jelly and Lolli drive in with Clive's car. The men jubilate…celebrating the arrival of Maputo.
They hug the girls and drink wine and beer.

Dialogue impro.

Cut to:

Scene 80:
Ext: crane shot/ms/sc
Rooftop of their building; Rita and Bobby discuss Zachy's problems and Bob Marley. They are eating pizzas.

Bobby:
I'm not sure what really happened but the police says he was driving a stolen car.

Rita:
Oh my God!...what has he done to himself?

Bobby:
I don't know…you know, Zachy is almost a nerd. He does his own thing and is a very private person.

Rita:
Where did the car come from?

Bobby:
I wouldn't know; I think it's from this man Iceman.

Rita:
Yo!...what a name…anyway, can we talk about Bob Marley…please?

Bobby:

What is it with you and the man; want to marry him or something?

Rita:
Say it again…possibly in the next life.
(They start to laugh)

Fade to Dark:

3 DAYS LATER

Scene 81:
Police station
Int: ms/mid/sc
Police holding cell; a police man enters and calls Zachy out; he
follows him to a corridor; they whisper; he follows him to a phone
booth…he picks the receiver and dials a number…he waits for a response.

Quick cut

Scene 82:
Ext: ms/mid/sc
Scrap yard…Iceman is walking around inspecting cars, his cellphone
rings; he checks caller ID, hesitates; answers

Iceman:
Talk, I'm listening

Zachy:
Ice…it's Zachy…please Bro. can you post my bail? I got bail this
morning and needs to get out of here.

Iceman: Still for a moment
Do you know what is called occam's razor Zach?

Zachy:
What?

Iceman:

Occam's razor…anyway don't worry. I'll see.

Cut to:

Scene 83:
Ext: ms/mid/cus
Bobby and Rita continue their dialogue on Bob Marley.

Bobby:
He moved to England on a self imposed exile for two years and produced some of his best tracks while he was there.

Rita:
Waoh!

Bobby:
Ya…songs "Exodus" that remained on the British charts for 56 straight weeks.

Rita:
You're lying

Bobby:
It's true; then "Kaya" and others and these marked the beginning of his career as an international artiste.

Rita:
Talk about winning against all odds.

Bobby:
Ya…the whole world began to take note of the man behind the most influential type of music then; one that was exclusively his.

Cut to:

Scene 84:

Ext/int: ls/mid/sc

The street to the police station; Fats and Tiny drive down the street, stops in front of the police station, parks, get out of the car and walk in.

Inside…they went to the counter and speak to the lady by the counter…

Tiny:
How are you Ma?

Police lady: looks up
Can I help you?

Tiny:
Yes please…we came to pick up a friend after posting his bail.

Police lady:
Where are the clearance papers?

He gives her a paper; she looks at it and at them too for seconds as if questioning them with her eyes.

Police lady:
Ok…take a seat; I'll go fetch him.

Fats:
You're so kind.

She gets up, stretches herself and begins to walk away casually.

Cut to:

Scene 85:
Int: ms/mid/sc
The studio…
The group plays African Jamaican Culure music, **"Ungodly Nation"**.

Song;
Jah Rastafar I

Ungodly nation,
Ungodly nation,
Why won`t you show mercy,
For Jah did show mercy upon you,

Why won`t you show mercy,
Unto the weak,
For He who have pity on the poor,
Lends to the Almighty God Jah Rastafar I,

For He shall pay back,
With what He has given,
Stop rebel against the truth,
For the violence of the wicked shall destroy them,

Because they refuse to do justice,
Oh, yee men of little faith,
Awake from your sleep and slumber,

Awake I say,

Why can`t you see
The victory of sons and daughters of the Most High,
His Imperial Majesty, Emperor King Rastafar I the Most High Haile
Selassie I,
You can`t beat them, So better join them

Ungodly nation,
Ungodly nation,
Why won`t you show mercy,
For Jah did show mercy upon you,

Why won`t you show mercy,
Unto the weak,
For He who have pity on the poor,

Lends to the Almighty God Jah Rastafar I,

For He shall pay back,
With what He has given,
Stop rebel against the truth,
For the violence of the wicked shall destroy them,

Because they refuse to do justice,
Oh, yee men of little faith,
Awake from your sleep and slumber,
Awake I say,

Why can`t you see
The victory of sons and daughters of the Most High,
His Imperial Majesty, Emperor King Rastafar I the Most High Haile
Selassie I,
You can`t beat them, So better join them

Oh yee men of little faith,
Awake from your sleep and slumber, awake I say,
Why can`t you scc,
The victory of sons and daughters,

Of the Most High, His Imperial Majesty,
Emperor King Rastafar I the Most High Haile Selassie I,
You can`t beat them,
So better join them

Make refuge in Him,
Before its too late,
For He is the great King of Glory,
Great King of Glory,

Rejoice not sons and daughters,
Because the rod that have strucked you is broken,
For out of the serpent root,
Will cometh forth a viper,

But rejoice the Lord Jah Rastafar I,
Has founded Zion and the poor of His people,
Shall take refuge in it, Glory and Praise,
Unto Thee Most High,

Oh yee men of little faith,
Awake from your sleep and slumber, awake I say,

Why can`t you see,
The victory of sons and daughters,

Of the Most High, His Imperial Majesty ,
Emperor King Rastafar I the Most High Haile Selassie I,
You can`t beat them,
So better join them

Make refuge in Him,
Before its too late,
For He is the great King of Glory,
Great King of Glory,

Rejoice not sons and daughters,
Because the rod that have strucked you is broken,
For out of the serpent root,
Will cometh forth a viper,

But rejoice the Lord Jah Rastafar I,
Has founded Zion,
And the poor of His people,
Shall take refuge in it,

Glory and Praise,
Unto Thee Most High,
Jah Rastafar I,
Jah Rastafar I,

None before
And none after,
King Haile Selassie I,

Jah Rastafar I Almighty I

[Guitar Cords; ||: Gm | F | Gm : || (2)
||: Cm | Cm | Gm | Gm :|| (1)
Guitar Solo; ||: Gm | F | Eb :|| (3)]

Slow fade

Scene 86:
Ext: ls/mid/sc
A lonely street, a posh car drives the down the street followed by
another car. It stops at a traffic light; Jelly gets out of the car behind points
a gun at the lady driver and orders her to come out.

Lolli comes from the opposite side, also gun trotting; the lady comes
out and begins to run away…she drops on the ground as Lolli and Jelly
drive away in her car.

Jelly: with a pointed gun
Get out lady

Lady: turns and sees her, eyes pops out, mouth open

Jelly: shouts at her
Get out of the car now

Lolli: shouts from her left side
What are you waiting for?
Get out…you want to die?

**She quickly opens the door, gets out and begins to run…drops on
the ground; the girls drive off in her car.**

Music continue playing

Cut to:

Scene 87:
Scrap yard

Int: ms/mid/sc

Iceman is irate and is shouting and threatening Zachy; the ladies drive in with the stolen car.

Iceman:

My man what were you thinking calling me from there? …you gone nuts or something?

Zachy:

Sorry Bro.. I didn't mean to put in harm's way. I needed help.

Iceman: calms down

By the way, how did it happen; were you flying or what?

Zachy: tries to reason with him

Come on Bossman…you know me. I don't drive like that. I guess he was just jealous.

Iceman:

Anyhow…I've no business with damn cops; I hate their guts because they are the greatest hypocrites ever.

Zachy:

Truly sorry Bro

The girls drive in…

Iceman: sees them

Aren't they the best? …not even you wasted muscles could do what they do.

Others look up…see the girls too and begin to clap.

They drive into the scrap yard…Iceman rushes to them; the rest follow.

Cut to:

Scene 88:

Int: ms/mid/sc

Bobby's flat; they are eating fruits; Bobby expressed desire to go to band practice; Rita promises to go with him if he tells him more about Bob Marley.

Bobby: standing by the kitchen stove, peeling apple with a knife.
I guess the men would be wondering what's going on.

Rita:
Ya... it's only natural.

Bobby:
I want to go up to the studio.

Rita:
Not a bad idea...when?

Bobby:
Now

Rita: reacts sharply
Now?

Bobby:
Ya...I'm not doing anything presently; except gossiping about Bob Marley.

Rita:
I disagree; we're not gossiping.

Bobby:
What do you call that?

Rita:
Knowledge transfer

Bobby:
Clever you **(His phone rings; its Zachy)**

Hei Zachy

Deep to black

Scene 89:
Another part of town
Ext: ls/mid/sc
Zach is walking along the road, talking to Bobby.

Zachy:
Where are you Bro?

Bobby: v/o
Home… and you?

Zachy:
Walking to the studio.

Bobby:
Waoh! … The man came good; happy meen!

Zachy:
Ya…thanks. Can we meet at the studio now?

Bobby:
Ya…I was actually thinking same; see you within the next 30.
(Drops the phone)

Rita:
Let me guess…Zachy

Bobby:
Yep…he's out

Rita:

Great…so what's the story?

Bobby:
Wants to meet at the studio…coming with?

Rita:
That won't hurt.

They get up and leave

Cut to:

Scene 90:
Ext: crane/ms/sc
Rooftop…the band meets up with Zachy; Bobby and Rita join. They kiss and hug each other and discuss what's happening.

Sly: hugs Zachy
Boy…what happened to you Bro. You just vanished, your phone was off, you're unreachable.

Zachy:
One of those things Bro. Cop issue.

Mercia: surprised
Cop issue…how?

Zachy:
Got arrested; they said the new car is stolen.

Rosey:
Sorry to hear that Big man

Tuffy:

Someone has to be covering your back Bro…I've always told you that.

Zachy:
Ya… I wish it was that easy.

Bobby and Rita enter

Bobby:
Hi people…Hi family

Rita stands aside smiling and watching them embrace each other,

Mercia: goes and hugs Rita
Heeii Rits…good that you came.
They all hug each other

Bobby: to Zachy
So what's next Zachy?

Zachy:
Time will tell

Bobby: raises his hand, to the rest
And to you family…what's for dinner?

They all start laughing.

Cut to:

NIGHT SKYLINE SHOTS

Next day

Scene 91:
Bobby's flat
Int: ms/mid/sc

He is with Rita…she gets up; goes and gets him a cup of coffee, makes one for herself, they drink and talk about Bob Marley as usual.

Rita: gets up, looks at Bobby; smiles and goes to the kitchen. Camera follows her there, she hums a song while making the coffee; takes it back to Bobby who is now awake…she greets.
Good morning love…**(gives him a cup of coffee, sits next to him and starts drinking hers….(asks)**

Is this the way Rita Marley treated her husband?

Bobby:
Now…that's a boggy question to ask. He had loads of other women and children so he had taste and choices.

Rita:
You mean outside marriage?

Bobby:
Ya…but he loved his wife till death and she was always with her in those trial times.

Rita:
And you?

Bobby:
Me what?

Rita:
Are you going to live that too?

Bobby:
Nope! …Perhaps that's where he's different from me; moreover women are too powerful and independent these days to allow such.

Rita:
So you dare not…**(points at him mockingly)**

ever…

Bobby:
Yes your worship

(They start to laugh)

Cut to:

Scene 92:
Another part of town…a street park
Ext: ls/ms/mid/sc
Lolli and Jelly sit on a bench at the park looking at passing cars;
suddenly another sleek car packs in front of a shop. They enter their car
and monitor it; the driver comes out from the shop with a plastic of
grocery, enters and drives off…they follow.

Dialogue impro

Play sound effects and line music
The car continues to speed and they follow unnoticed.

Cut to:

Scene 93:
Fast food outlet
Ext: ms/mid/sc
Bobby and Rita sit outside the fast food outlet eating and talking
about Bob Marley.

Bobby:
He really became a world music icon and was at the height of his
career when a dodgy ailment attacked him.

Rita:
What was that?

Bobby:
Some say he had a wound on his toe that refused to heal; intense tests later revealed that it was malignant melanoma and needed amputating the toe but he refused.

Rita:
Why

Bobby:
Because he was a Rastafarian and such was against our culture; others claimed it would've negatively affected his dancing skills.

Rita:
So he allowed it to kill him?

Bobby:
The reasoning was beyond me.

Rita:
That was crazy…was what killed him?

Cut to:

Scene 94:
Ext: ls/mid/sc
Back on the road; Jelly and Lolli are still following the car. The car stops in front of a house; the occupant gets out and enters the house. They park down the street in an opposite lane.

Cut to:

Scene 95:
Scrap yard
Int/ext: ms/mid/sc
Iceman oversees the cars being broken down flanked by Tiny and fats.
He calls Lolli

Cut to:

Scene 96:
Ext: ls/mid/sc
Anonymous Street...
Lolli and jelly are sitting in their car waiting for a prey. Lolli's phone rings; she answers.

Lolli:
Hi Ice

v/o:
Where are you?

Lolli:
On an assignment; we'll be back soon.

v/o:
Please be careful...alright?

Lolli:
Are you ok?

Iceman:
Ya...I just got this cold chill.

Lolli: emotional
Shame...I'll be fine...you know how it is.

Iceman:
If you say so...tell Jelly what I said ok? ...see you people.

Lolli:
I will ...bye
(Turns to Jelly)
Is Iceman turning into a grandmother or what?

Jelly:
What happened?

Lolli:
He's worried about us and wants us to be careful

Jelly:
I feel the same way too…anyhow, this is our last job for the year.

A lady comes out from the house and goes towards the packed car.

Lolli sees her and gets out of the car.

I'll take this Jell …(she follows the lady asking her to wait, the lady turns, sees her and stands next to the car; Jelly is glued to her seat in shock at how fast Lolli is)
(She gets to the lady; engages her in a short discussion, Lolli draws a gun; two shots rang out immediately; she drops to the ground, Jelly gets out of their own car and runs towards her…the car drives off.
She gets to Lolli, goes down and carries her bleeding forehead…
Blood is dripping from her mouth and stomach.

Lolli: her eyes weak, she looks at Jelly, mutters incoherent words, blood oozing from her mouth and wounds.
My baby… my baby **(dies)**

Jelly lets out a huge yell, a thickly bearded man in glasses dressed in a sports gear riding a sports bicycle stops to help…gets down next them, touches Jelly by the shoulder; she look at him.
(Mid to C.U shot of the two looking at each other)

Quick fade to Dark.

1 MONTH LATER

Shot of Johannesburg rising. A Street in a quiet suburb; a couple dressed in sports gear rides on a sports bike down the road.

Scene 97:
Ext: ls/mid/sc
They stop in front of a nicely built house; gate opens and they walk in. The man puts his bike inside the booth of his car; hugs the woman, they kiss and he enters the car and drives off.
The woman stands and looks at the car driving away.
Slow close up shot of her face reveals she is Jelly.

M.O.D…Play sound effects

Cut to:

Scene 98:
Bobby's flat
Int: ms/mid/sc
Bobby is sitting on a couch drinking coffee; Rita dressed in a see-through clothes comes out from the bathroom…goes and sits next to him; takes his left hand in hers.

Rita: tries to look him in the eyes
Baby…

Bobby:
What's going on? …you've been acting strange the whole morning.

Rita:
Sorry…it feels strange to me too.

Bobby:
What is strange?...are you ok Baby?
(Fully concerned now)

Rita:
I've never been better; it's you I'm worried about.

Bobby:
What's going on…stop speaking in tongue please?

Rita:
I'm worried about how you'd react to this.

Bobby: worried now
To what? …now I'm really worried.

Rita: brings out a pregnancy test kit; shows him.
To this…I am pregnant

Quick cut

Scene 99:
Exclusive part of town
Ext: ms/mid/sc
Our newest couple, Clive and Casandra is sitting outside a Bistro in Melville having lunch; his phone beeps a message sound, he checks it out and exclaims in joy.

Clive: joyfully
Yes…yes…yes (punching the air)

Caz: shocked
What happened?... a fairly good news I suppose?

Clive:
You can say that again; the shares I've been tracking for a while now has matured due to consistent drop in oil prices over these periods.

Caz: confused, shakes her head as if seeking for answers
Meaning?

Clive:
Meaning I can now sell to the highest bidder for over 700% gain

Caz:
You're joking right?

Clive:
I don't joke with business Caz. I love making money classically; making money while having fun.

Caz: fully interested
Please teach me…I am sick and tired of what I do.

Clive:
You know…you've not really told me about it.

Caz:
What is there to tell…it makes my heart bleed.

Clive:
Then why do it?

Caz:
What choice do I have?

Clive:
There are choices always; the challenge is for us to make positive ones.

Caz:
You know…I once met a Clive and he was cool as well. Are you people always this cool; I mean Clives?

Clive:
Where did you people meet?

Caz:
It's a long story

Clive:
We've got time…plenty of it

Her phone rings; she checks out the caller ID.

Caz:
Hello Ice … alright I'm coming.
(Excuses herself)
Please excuse me for about twenty (20) minutes. I need to see a friend
of mine urgently.

Clive:
Want me to come with?

Caz:
No…it's an all woman thing. Please… **(Takes his hands).** I'll be
back before you say Caz.

Clive: hesitates
Ok…if you say so

Caz: Gives him a peck on the cheek
Thank you…I apologize.
(Gets up)

Clive: stands up too
Shall I walk you to your car?

Caz:
No need…I'll call you once I'm done.
(Walks away)

(Slow zoom in on Clive's face).

Clive: soliloquy v/o

Is this not Jelly; one of the ladies that stole my car... could she be this sweet and civil. She's been a very ideal companion since we met under that bizarre circumstance. ...Come to think of it, was that a deal gone wrong or an accident as she claims...I must find out. God help her if she is.

Cut to:

Scene 100:
Ext: crane/mid/sc
Bobby and Rita are sitting on the rooftop with Zachy. Zachy's phone rings and he leaves.

Rita:
How many children did Bob Marley have?

Bobby:
I think about twelve (12) or slightly more.

Zachy:
And that would include adopted ones too

Rita:
How many mothers or shall I say women.

Bobby:
About three or four that had his children including Rita, his legitimate wife. Others could not be established.

Zachy:
Why all these question about children and stuff?

Bobby:
Because we are expecting our own.

Zachy: shouts
Waoh! ...Congratulations people; its really a milestone.
(His phone rings, he checks out called ID and takes his exit quickly)
See you people later.

Bobby: comments
Zachy and his deals.

Cut to:

Scene 101:
Scrap yard
Int: ms/mid/sc
Iceman is trying to cajole Jelly now Caz into a relationship and life with him while they maintain their business. The two are locked in his office at the scrap yard.
They are drinking wine and talking.

Caz:
With all due respects Ice; you are crazy to even suggest that.

Iceman:
Is marrying me that terrible?

Caz:
How can you even think of it; even suggest it, it is the craziest proposal I can think of and I think it's selfish of you to ask me that.

Iceman:
Who is he?

Caz:
Who is who?

Iceman:
Who is the new man?

Caz:
Look Ice…this is really strange, you've never expressed any romantic interest in me all these years, not the slightest of it; suddenly you woke up this morning and your heart told you that I am the one for you…how daft.

Iceman:
Ok… are we still on?

Caz:
No Ice…I am done; you should be done too. Lolli's death should've told you so. My name is Casandra; no more Jelly, Lolli or those crazy names. The crazy times are over.

(she turns and begins to walk away; picks her phone from her handbag, makes a phone call as she continues walking)

Iceman: Yells after her
Who is the man Jell?
(instructs Tiny and Fats to follow her discreetly)
hei! **(Points to the two)**
Find out what's going on… now.
(They rush out, jump into a car and drive off after her).

Cut to:

Scene 102:
Exclusive part of town
Ext: ls/ms/mid/sc
Clive sits on his own, his hands carrying an almost full glass of brandy…he thinks about Caz.

Clive: soliloquy

How do I handle this scenario? I am almost sure this is Jelly; the woman that stole my car with her friend.

Quick dissolve

Scene 103:
Same loc
Ext: ms/mid/sc
Clive continues
How can I be this cozy with a woman that nearly killed me. How am I even sure she's the same woman; she seem so different, so perfect, so innocent and incapable to do something that inhuman.

He takes a sip, exhales and looks straight
How do I handle the truth if it turns out that way?. Take my revenge? Kill her? Hand her over to the cops?

His phone rings; he picks it; checks the caller ID…answers

Hi…

v/o:
Where are you…I'm done?

Clive:
Still here

v/o:
Still there? It's over an hour now.

Clive:
Yeah! Lost track of time.

v/o:
I'm on my way

Cut to:

Scene 104:

Bobby's flat
Int: ms/mid/sc
Bobby and Rita are cooking together in the kitchen.

Rita:
I think it's time you people let Zachy go or he'll put all of you in trouble.

Bobby:
Why do you think so?

Rita:
His life style is questionable to say the least.

Bobby:
Because of the arrest?...it can happen to anyone. The band is bigger than any of us as an individual so if all of us feel anyone is badly influencing the brand we're trying to build, we'll leave the person.

Rita:
Guaranteed?

Bobby:
I cross my heart.

Cut to:

Scene 105:
Another part of town
Ext: ls/mid/sc
Caz is driving along the road; Fats and Tiny follows in a distance to shield themselves from her.
(She thinks of Clive)

Caz v/o:
Clive… who is this man?

There's something about him that makes me very uncomfortable but I can't seem to put my finger on it.

Long shot shows Tiny and Fats following Jelly now Caz.

Caz v/o:
He is so much like that Clint man and I hope I'm wrong…what the hell…who cares anymore; whatever happens, happens

Long shot…she drives down the street, followed by Fats and Tiny; turns a corner, parks in front of a bistro and comes out.

P.O.V shot…Caz hugs Clive, they sit, Fats and Tiny watch from a long distance…Caz is oblivious of the two of them watching them.
Fats calls Iceman to report…

Fats: while watching the two, he dials Iceman.
Right on point Boss, there's a bloody goat.

Quick dissolve

Scene 106:
Int: ms/mid/sc
Scrap yard

Iceman:
Who's the damn goat?

Fats: v/o
I don't know him Big man
(Looks at Tiny with questioning eye; he responds in the negative)
Tiny doesn't know him too.

Iceman:
Find out who he is, what he wants and where he's from; we'll pay him a visit.

Fats: v/o
Will do Boss…will do

Long shot
Clive and Caz get up; he walks her to her car; she enters and drives
off. Tiney and Fats enter their own car as he watches Caz drive off; he
enters his car and drives off; they follow.

Cut to:

Scene 107:
Ext: ls/ms/mid/sc
Another part of town… the shrine. It's celebrations and the band is
there in full swing.
Bobby is doing a **African Jamaican Culture song,"Roots of Haile
Selassie I Rastafari"**, Rita and her friends dance and cheer for him. It was
birthday anniversary of Emperor Haile Selassie I, our God incarnate;
people are celebrating.

Song;
Roots of Haile Selassie I Rastafari
The Royal blood line of A Sheba
This is how the seed of Abraham return
I ya exalt Him that rideth upon the heavens by his name JAH
RASTAFARI
And rejoice before Him

Give ear to my words, Oh King of kings Haile Selassie I
Consider my meditation

Thy word is a light unto I Rastafari
The baldhead shall melt in the flame
For Thou teacheth I wisdom

Yea though I walk through the valley of the shadow of death

I will fear no evil for thou art with I
Thy rod and thy staff they comfort I

So I ya rejoice
I ya rejoice
I ya rejoice
I ya rejoice

I ya rejoice O
I ya rejoice O
I ya rejoice O
I ya rejoice O
I ya rejoice O O

I ya rejoice O
I ya rejoice O

I ya rejoice O
I ya rejoice O

I ya rejoice O O
I ya rejoice
I ya rejoice
I ya rejoice O

Thy word is a light unto I Rastafari
The baldhead shall melt in the flame
For Thou teacheth I wisdom

Yea though I walk through the valley of the shadow of death
I will fear no evil for thou art with I

I ya rejoice O
I ya rejoice
I ya rejoice
I ya rejoice O

I ya rejoice O
I ya rejoice

I ya rejoice
I ya rejoice O

**(Guitar Cords; D | G- | D | F
H- | G | F)**

Rita:
What is all this about?

Bobby:
We celebrate the birthday of our founding father, **Emperor Haile Selassie I of Ethiopia**…the only African leader never to be colonized by the West.

Rita:
Waoh! …so this thing started in Ethiopia.

Bobby:
First of all, it is not this thing; It is a way of life, culture, history.

Rita:
Sorry

Bobby:
Ya…just like the development of reggae is a part of I and I culture

Rita:
I understand now; where is Zachy?

Bobby:
I don't know…you know he does his own things.

Zachy is not there, he's gone to the Scrap yard to meet Iceman and discuss his court case.

Scene 108:
Another part of town…
Int: ms/mid/sc
Scrap yard, Zachy is with Iceman, he wants him to pay for his court case in exchange for his silence. Iceman agrees but then decides that Zachy must be killed because he has become a big liability and threat.

Zachy:
I really need your help Ice…I need money to sort out my lawyer and I don't have it.

Iceman:
What a shame…when is the court case?

Zachy:
Tomorrow morning and my lawyer said he's not coming if he doesn't get the money; I've called and pleaded with you to pay me my money…

Iceman: Raises his voice, cuts him off
Hei! Hei! Hei!...who are you talking to like that?...are you mad? (points at him; tries to bully him)
Don't you ever… do you hear me; ever talk to me in that manner.

Zachy: angry
If I don't get the money; I will be forced to talk and you wouldn't want that…please give me the money.

Iceman looks at him ice cold for a couple of seconds.
v/o:
rat on me?...nobody does that Zachs; you've just signed your death warrant and I am sorry you have to die in this manner…

(Puts up a sinister smile, holds him by the shoulder in a friendly manner and asks him to come with him).

Iceman:
It's ok …come; come with me; let's organize you some money.
(He throws his hand on his shoulder and they walk to the back yard).

Cut to:

Scene 109:
Another part of town…
Ext: ls/mid/sc
Clive drives stops in front of a remote controlled gate; it opens and he drives in. Fats and Tiny drives past him; stops and picks up the address and drives away.

Cut to:

Scene 110:
Scrap yard
Ext: ms/mid/sc

Back yard…Iceman takes Zachy to the back of the compound and pulls out a gun….his tone and expression turns cold and menacing for Zachy to start panicking, apologizing.

Iceman:
You are a good boy Zachy…you were a good boy…now, you decided to kill yourself; why? (cynical)

Zachy:
I'm sorry Iceman; I would never do that; its just that this case is making me crazy and I'm trying everything I could to make it go away.

Iceman:
By ratting on your Boss?

Zachy:
I would never have done that; please don't kill me.

Iceman:
You don't rat on your Boss no matter the situation…(Points the gun at him)
Now look at what you've made me do.

Zachy: raises both hands; goes into a frenzy
Please don't kill me

Dissolve

Scene 111:
Another part of town
Ext: ls/wide/mid/sc
Fats and Tiny are driving along the road towards the scrap yard; Fats calls Iceman.

Fats: dials Iceman

Quick dissolve

Scene 112:
Back at the scrap yard
Int: ms/mid/sc
Iceman's phone rings; he looks at the caller ID…answers.

Iceman:
Yes

Fats: v/o
Hei Boss…we're on the way back.

Iceman:

Meaning work done

Zachy begins to walk away slowly.

Fats: v/o
100%

Zachy continues walking away

Enter sound effects

Iceman:
Great… get back here; we have a shit to clean up and go to see the idiot later.

Fats v/o:
We'll be there in five Boss.

P.O.V shot…

Zachy turns to run; a shot goes off; he drops to the ground.

Slow zoom-in shot

Close up shot of Zachy lying on the ground in a pool of blood…he is dead.

Fats and Tiny enter…see the body. Rude shock on their faces.
Iceman: points at Zachy
That's the shit to clean up; we go see the bastard later.
(Begins to walk away)

Fats: calls out to him
Boss

Iceman: talks on his way out
He wanted to rat…threatened to rat. Cover him up there…dump him after dark.

Cut to:

Scene 113:
Another part of town
Int: ms/mid/sc
Bobby's flat
He is in bed with Rita; they kissed.

Rita:
Why do I love you so much?

Bobby: jokingly
Because you love me.

Rita: hits him softly
Naughty you…you know; you didn't tell me when and how he died.

Bobby:
Who died?

Rita:
Who else?…Bob Marley.

Bobby:
Ok…yes…

Rita:
But before that…what about this other man; Haile Selassie I?

Bobby:
What about him too?

Rita:
What happened to him?

Bobby:
Haile Selassie I live forever;

He ruled his country, led his people like me till they told us he was killed by his nephew for power.

Rita:
What a shame…and Bob Marley?

Cut to:

LATER THAT EVENING

NIGHT

Scene 114:
Another part of town…
Clive's house
Int: ms/mid/sc
He is at home with Caz; they are seated in the lounge seeping wine and making small talks. A bell rings, he goes to check.

Clive:
You know, it has really been a whirlwind since we met.

Caz:
Say it again…you're really and truly a great man; gorgeous to say the least and I wonder what you're doing with somebody like me.

Clive:
Why is that?

Caz:
There are few good men around and I strongly believe that you're one of them; hanging out with someone like me seems like an aberration.

Clive:
Why is that again? …is it because Caz is bad or Jelly; which of the two.

Caz: shocked to her roots; panicky
She nearly spilled her drink.
What? …what are talking about?

Clive:
You know very well Jelly

Caz:
Then why am I here?

Clive: Goes to her, kisses her fully on the mouth.
Because I'm in love with you…at least I think so; or would like to believe so.

Caz: sits up
You can't be serious…(stands)
I stole your car and left you for dead.
You could've been dead for all I care.
What kind of love is that?

Clive:
I knew it was you that day we met again under the painful circumstance but was not very sure.

Caz:
So you had to find out?

Clive:
Yes…but I knew you didn't do it for yourselves.

Caz:
What are you going to do with me?

Clive:
Who is he?

Cut to:

Scene 115:
Int: ms/mid/sc
Bobby's flat
They're still in bed
He talks about Bob Marley as usual

Bobby:
They killed Bob Marley and told us that
Bob Marley died on the 11th of May 1981 in Miami, Florida U.S.A. at the age of 36 from what the doctors called Metastatic Skin Cancer.

Rita:
Oh God!...what a shame; but why is he still popular till today.

Bobby:
Because Rastafarians never die; He was the greatest Jah Rastafari prophet and Reggae musician that ever lived and one of the greatest modern musicians of our times along the likes of Elvis Presley and Michael Jackson.

Rita:
I agree

Bobby:
Some say Bob Marley allowed a little toe cancer to grow and destroy his whole body because of his deep-rooted culture and it killed him years later.

Rita:
I wonder why he did that?

Bobby:
Bob Marley live;
That will show you the kind of man he was. Moreover he believed he will live forever through his music therefore he was not afraid of death, how true he was,

Cut to:

Scene 116:
Another part of town
Clive's house
Int: ms/mid/sc
His dialogue with Caz continue.

Caz:
Who is who?

Clive:
Who is the man that led you people to that?...you and your late friend. I am sure it was why she died.

Caz: reacts sharply
Did you kill Lolli?

Clive: Goes to her again, urges her to sit down, sits next to her, takes her hand, looks into her eyes.
Look Casandra...I've no reason to do that. I've no reason to kill you either. All I want is to free you from the bondage...help you because I love

you…Love at first sight they call it; it happened that first time we met but you disappointed me.

Caz: takes away her hand gently
We were under the influence and were sent to it. We've stopped though; unfortunately my friend died in our last hit…and for what?
All to satisfy the greed of one man.
Not my man though.

Clive: Takes back her hand
I can help you purge your conscience and sense of guilt; let's bring the man down. Let's end this once and for all. Take your life back and be free to have a life with me.

Caz:
You're unbelievable…can I kiss you?

The gate bell rings; he gets up to go get it.

Clive: goes to know who's there.
Hold that kiss…I want it and more.

Caz sits and waits in amazement; she couldn't believe what's happening.

Deep to black

Show night street shots; introduce special sound effects depicting approaching danger.

Enter…

Scene 117:
Clive's house
Int: ms/mid/sc
Clive walks back into the lounge on his back; both hands are raised as Iceman points a gun at his face.

Caz sees them and jumps up from her seat and rushes and stands in front of him.

Caz: shocked to see them, rushes to Clive.
What?...how did you find me? ...what are you doing here?...Ice?...what's going on?

Iceman: his gun still pointed at Clive
Shut up Jell
(Orders Tiny and Fats to tie them up)
Tie them up

Tiny:
Both of them Boss?

Iceman: shouts at him
Yes...you idiot

Fats and Tiny ties Clive and Caz up.

Caz: to Tiny
What are you doing T?

Tiny: mutters silently
Sorry; it's not tight

Clive: distracts Iceman's attention while being tied up by Fats.
So...this is the monster that took my car?

Iceman:
What are you talking?...what did you say?

Clive:
You are the man behind all these brutalities?

Iceman:

Which brutalities…look if I were you, I'll shut up and not provoke me; not that it will save you anyway.

Caz: To Iceman
Ice; when did it get to this?

Iceman:
When you decided to disobey me and do as you wished…(asks)
Who is this damn man?
Your new man now?

Caz:
You're crazy

Iceman laughs; orders Fats and Tiny to bring them along.

Iceman:
Men bring the fools…let's go

Caz:
Where are you taking us…what has he done?

Iceman: Ignores her
Let's go
(They go; he follows behind them with his gun pointed; on second thought, he leaves Caz behind.

Iceman:
On second thought, let Jell wait for us here; leave her behind, get her phones, we'll come back for her later.

Tiny takes her back in.

Scene 118:
Clive's lounge
Int: ms/mid

Tiny:
It's not too tight…save yourself.

Caz:
Where are you people going?

Tiny:
Not sure…possibly the scrap yard
(Runs out)

Cut to:

Scene 119:
Another part of town
Bobby's flat
Int: ms/mid/sc
Bobby and Rita is making love under a covered sheet.

Cut to:

Scene 120:
Another part of town
Scrap yard
Ext: ms/mid/sc
Zachy's body lies outside amongst the mangled bodies of cars.

Cut to:

Scene 121:
Same scrap yard
Int: ms/mid/sc

Clive is tied to a chair, Iceman sits opposite him cutting an apple with a knife while watching Fats pummel Clive who is bleeding all over.

Iceman:
You think you can butt into our lives and destroy everything I've worked for all my life.

Clive:
What have I done to you…what did I do?

Iceman: gives Fats a sign, he punches him.

You don't touch my woman…do you hear me?...you don't dare walk into my world without my permission.

Clive:
But I don't know you; I just met the woman and we're just friends, nothing more than that.

Iceman:
Too late to cry when the head is already off.

Clive:
You're going to kill me for doing nothing to you?

Cut to:

Scene 122:
Another part of town
Clive's house…lounge
Int: ms/mid/sc
Caz is busy untying the rope
She unties it; takes her handbag, brings out a gun…walks out as if in a trance.

Cut to:

Montage shot…night time in Jozi

Scene 123:
Back at the scrap yard
Int: ms/mid/sc
Same scenario;

Clive:
Only cowards use others to do their dirty jobs. I've done nothing to you; if you want to kill me, do it yourself and now, leave these victims out.

Iceman: jumps from the chair and slaps him hard in the face.
Don't ever talk to me like that.

Clive:
Or what?...you'll kill me?...you stupid fool. You want me to crawl on my knees and beg that you spared me life.
(Taunts him)

You're a bloody coward; you think life is all about destroying others to live.

Iceman: irate (Fats and Tiny watches in consternation)
Shut up you fool...**(raging)**
You don't know anything about me you idiot.

Clive:
Really... I do not need magic to see how useless you are. You think the world owns you; that is why you are killing and destroying. You think you have a right to spill blood; as if you created it.

Iceman: Looses it, flares into a rage
Shut up

Clive:
Remove these ropes

Iceman: shouting on top of his voice, covers his ears with both hands including the one holding the gun.
Shut up

Clive:
Untie me…we live in a free country.

Iceman:
Shut up…you idiot..you don't know me…you don't know my life…what I've been through; how hard, how rough, how wicked, how deadly, how…**(Shouts again)** shut up

Clive:
I can help you.

Iceman: flares into continued rage
Help me…help me **(Points the gun at him)** what would you do for me? Ehee? …give me millions? …make me a millionaire?...you bloody idiot.

(Takes aim)
Good bye mother fucker

A shot rings out

Change of shot…wide / P.O.V

Iceman's eyes pops out in shock, he opens his mouth to talk but chokes, blood flowing from his mouth.
Caz walks in wielding a gun, he sees her; his expressions changes.

Iceman:
You…
(Drops to the floor)
Fats tries to run, she shoots him too **(He drops).**
Quick flashbacks
Scene 124:
Ms
Dead body of Zachy where it is lying

Scene 125:
Ms
Dead body of Lollipop lying on the street after she was shot mysteriously.

Scene 126:
Ms
Lolli and Jell rob a woman of her car at an intersection.

Scene 127:
Ms
Lolli and Jell rob Clive, then Clint of his car leaving him in the bushes.

Scene 128:
Ms
All of them celebrating delivery of Clive's car then.

Scene 129:
Same Loc.
Ms
Tiny raises both hands; Caz asks him to relax; they both untie Clive; she tells Tiny to go.

He refuses and wants to help; she shouts at him to go while busy cleaning Clive's wounds.
She takes her cellphone and calls the police.

Caz:
Hello…is that 10111…I just killed two (2) men…address is 22 Kotze Street Roodeporte.

She helps Clive get up and they walk away with him holding her shoulders and limping.

ENDS